AF390057

How To Draw Cute Food

Step by Step Instructions with Art Grids

By

Amber Forrest

No part of this publication may be reproduced or transmitted in any form whatsoever, electronic, or mechanical, including photocopying, recording, or by any informational storage or retrieval system without express written, dated and signed permission from the author.

©Copyright 2019 – Amber Forrest.
ALL RIGHTS RESERVED.

Published By:

Amber Forrest

Website : www.amberforrest.com

ISBN: 978-81-945129-5-0

HEY... THANK YOU FOR BEING AWESOME.

WE HOPE THAT YOU HAVE FUN TIME WITH YOUR BOOK. WE HAVE GIFT FOR YOU. YOU CAN DOWNLOAD A FREE PRINTABLE SET OF OUR BEST COLORING PAGES BY VISITING OUR WEBSITE :

AMBERFORREST.COM

IT WOULD BE SO COOL IF YOU COULD SHARE YOUR COMPLETED IMAGES WITH US. YOU CAN TAG US ON

FACEBOOK & INSTAGRAM
@COLORWITHAMBER

WE ARE ALWAYS WORKING HARD TO IMPROVE OUR BOOKS. PLEASE LET US KNOW HOW WE ARE DOING BY WRITING A REVIEW OF OUR BOOK ON YOUR FAVORITE ONLINE STORE.

INTRODUCTION

Drawing is a learned skill, one built over years of consistent practice. If you have the passion and commitment, you can take your knack for scribbling in the margins to a dedicated drawing practice. Figuring out where to begin and what to draw can be challenging. But you have to start drawing somewhere, and you can start where you are, with this book in your hand.

In this book you will find step-by-step illustrations to help you draw. You can also take the help of art grids if you find it difficult to draw proportionately. Anytime you want to draw something that requires accuracy (a portrait, a pet, a vehicle, a complex still life), you might want to use the grid method. It allows you to break the reference down into smaller and more manageable segments. Even the best artists in the world will struggle to draw complex objects purely by eye, without any visual aid like construction lines.

There's no avoiding it: learning to draw well takes practice. Don't worry about any mistakes you make along the way. Every single bit of effort counts. There is no such thing as wasted effort in drawing. So just..

"Practice, practice, practice, and don't give up."

SUPER APPLE

Step by Step Instructions

Draw inside the box with the help of art grids.

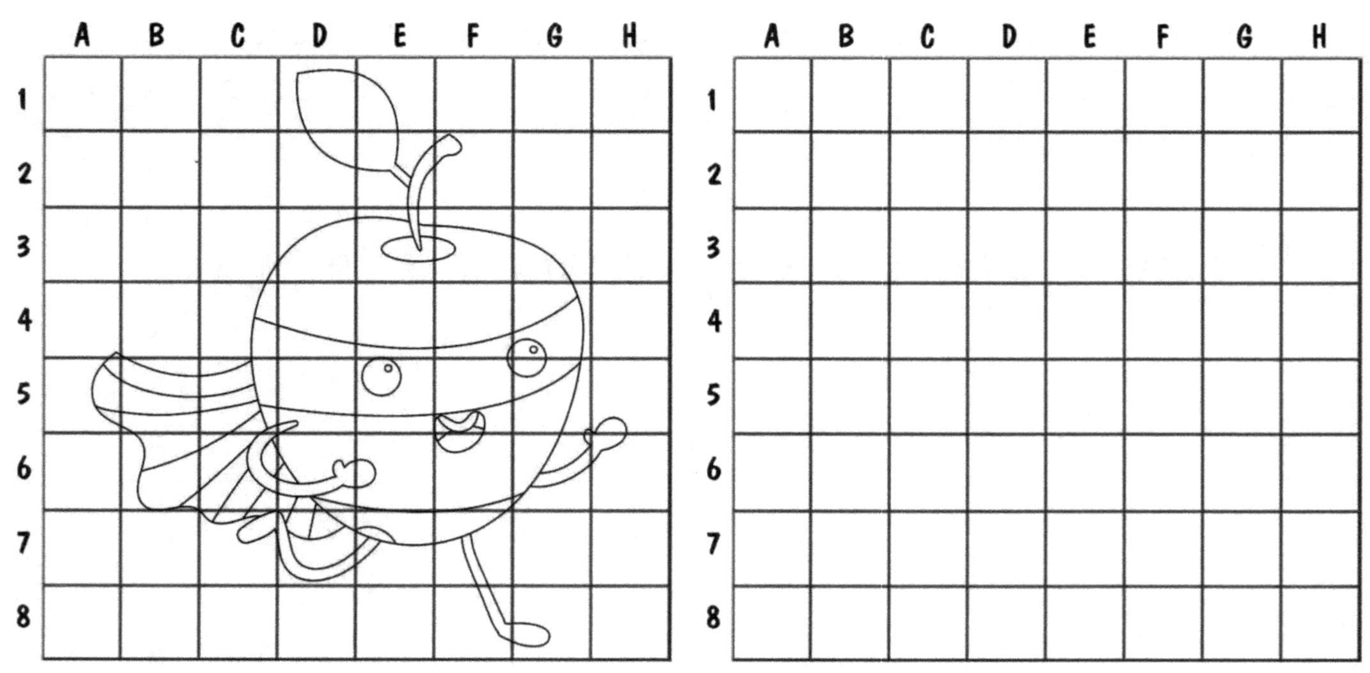

NOW COLOR IT

YOUR TURN TO DRAW

SUPER BANANA

Step by Step Instructions

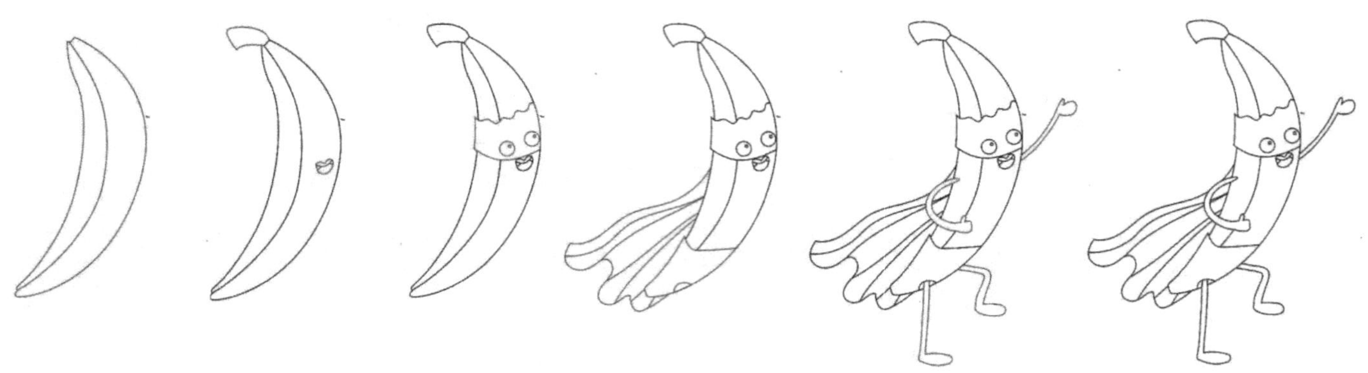

Draw inside the box with the help of art grids.

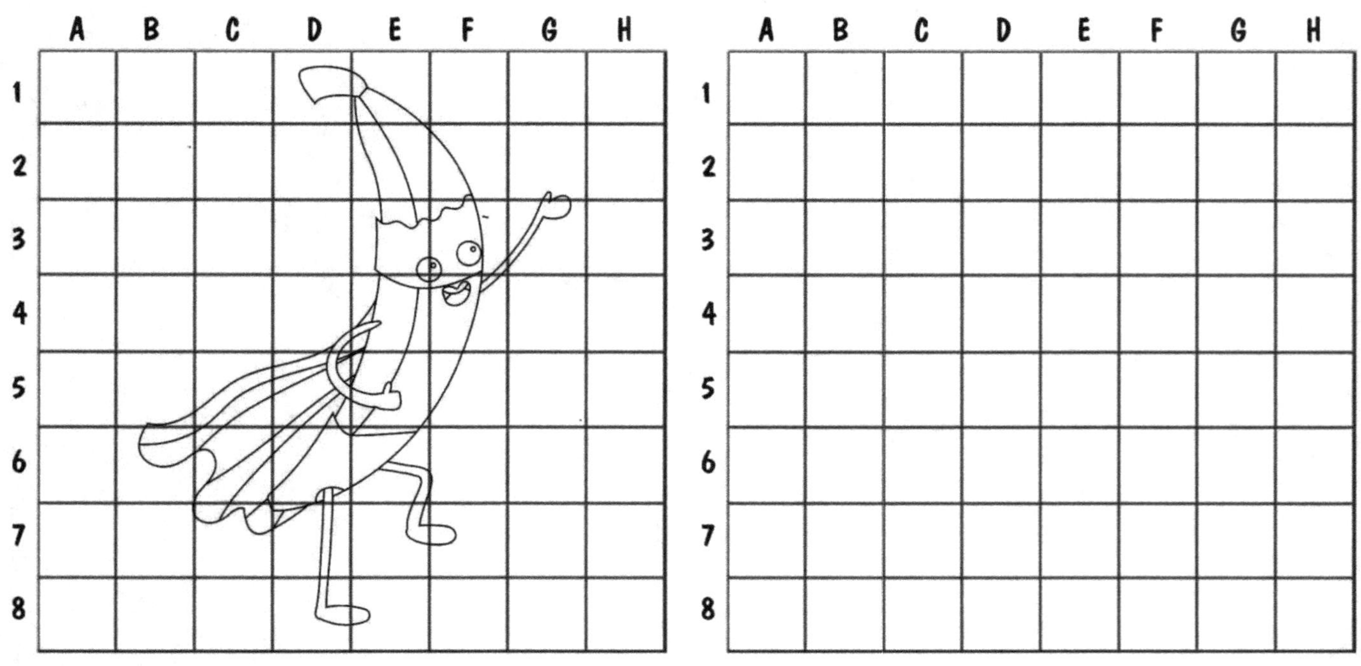

NOW COLOR IT

YOUR TURN TO DRAW

SUPER LEMON

Step by Step Instructions

Draw inside the box with the help of art grids.

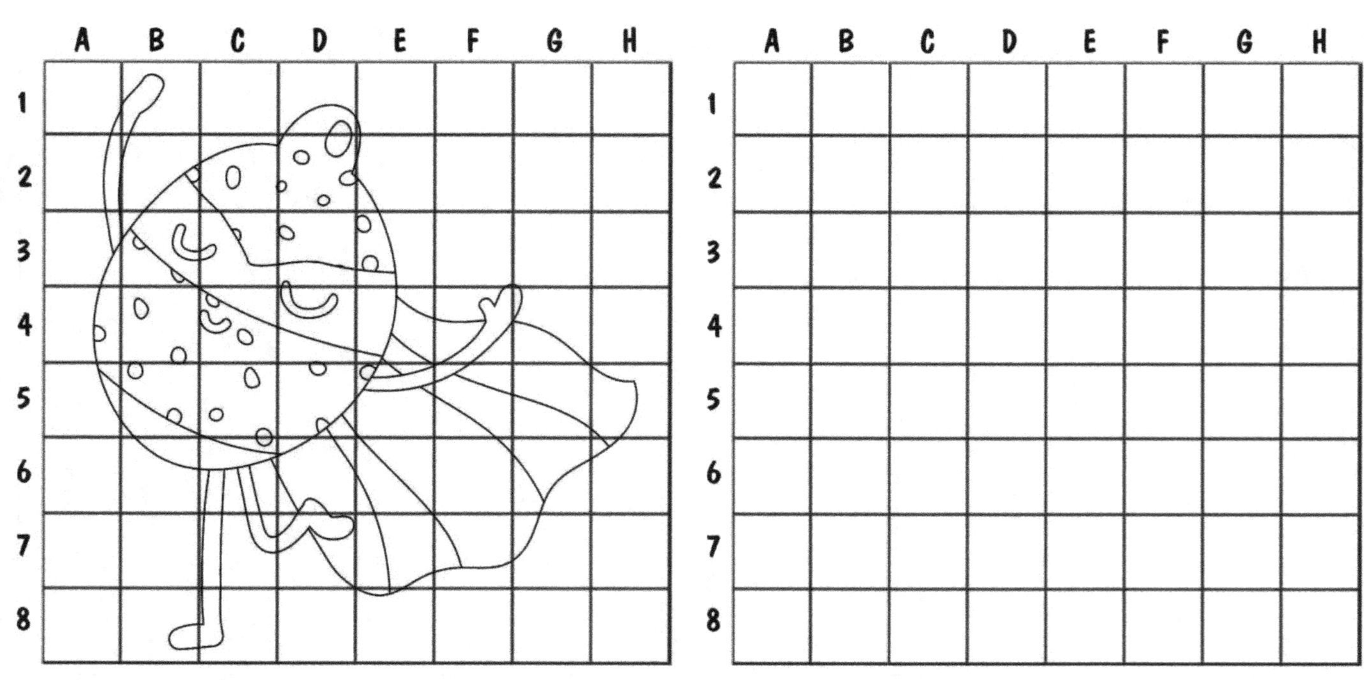

NOW COLOR IT

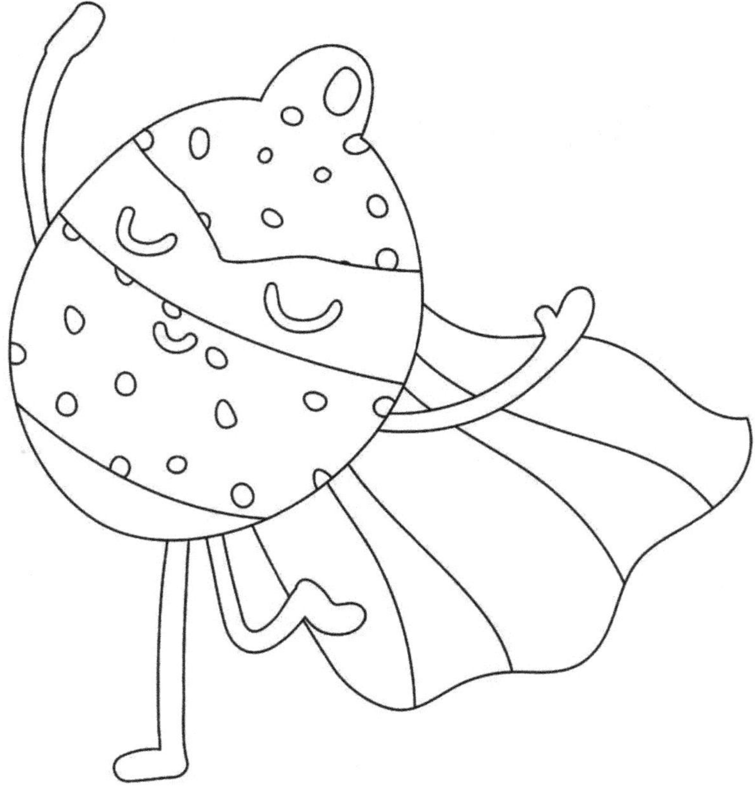

YOUR TURN TO DRAW

SUPER ORANGE

Step by Step Instructions

Draw inside the box with the help of art grids.

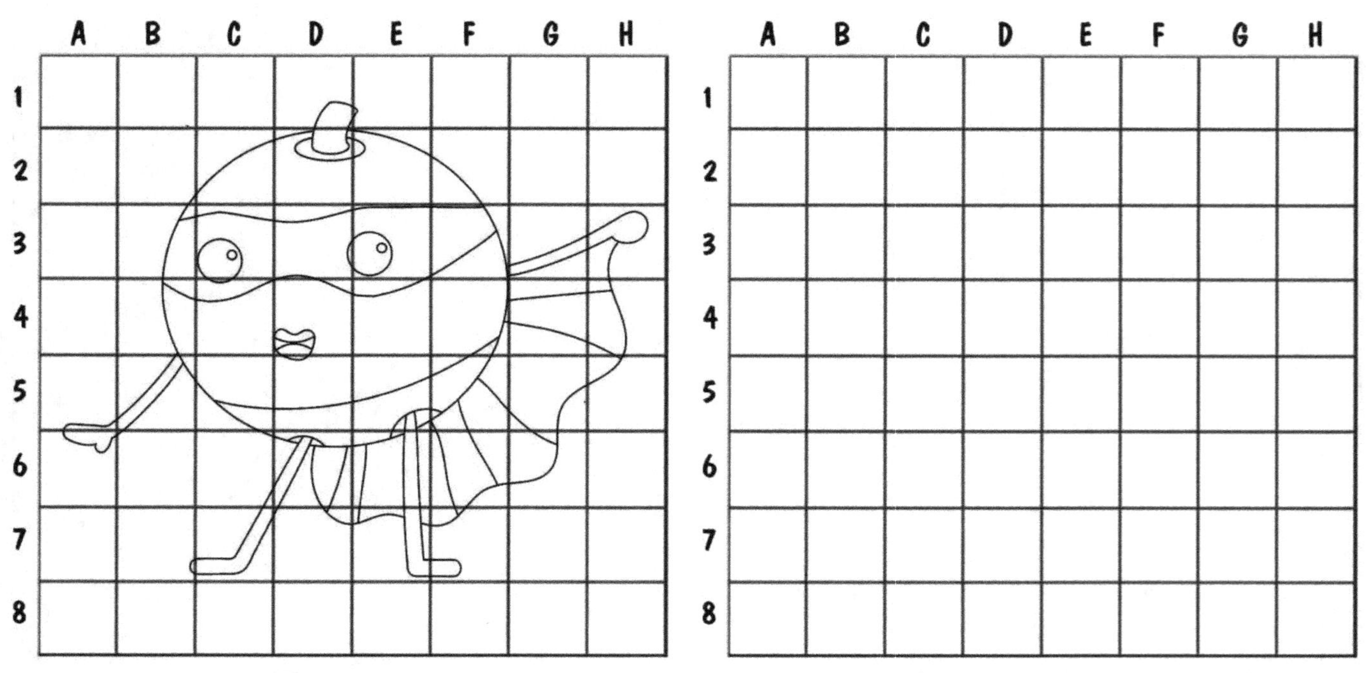

NOW COLOR IT

YOUR TURN TO DRAW

SUPER PEAR

Step by Step Instructions

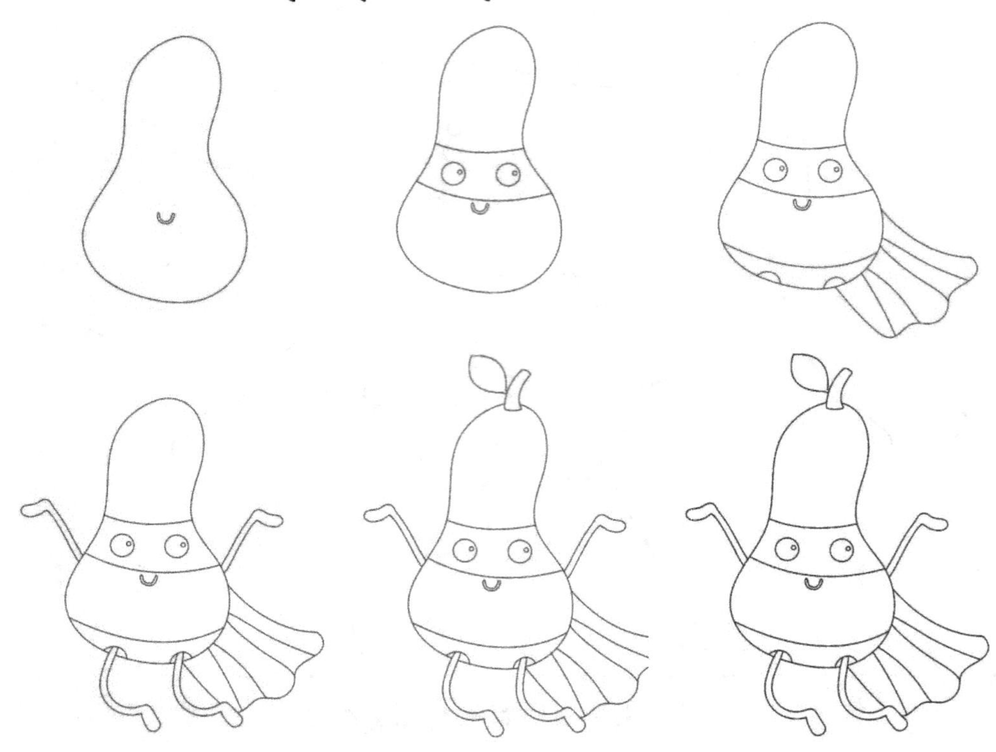

Draw inside the box with the help of art grids.

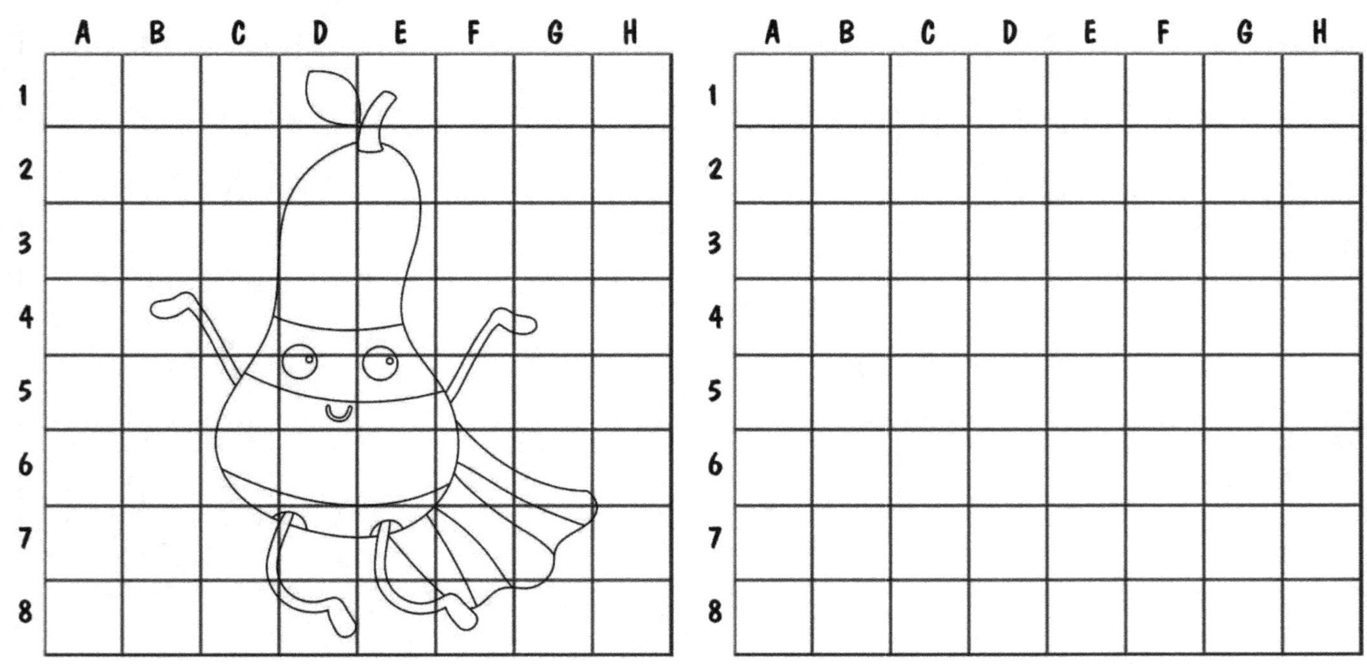

NOW COLOR IT

YOUR TURN TO DRAW

SUPER PINEAPPLE
Step by Step Instructions

Draw inside the box with the help of art grids.

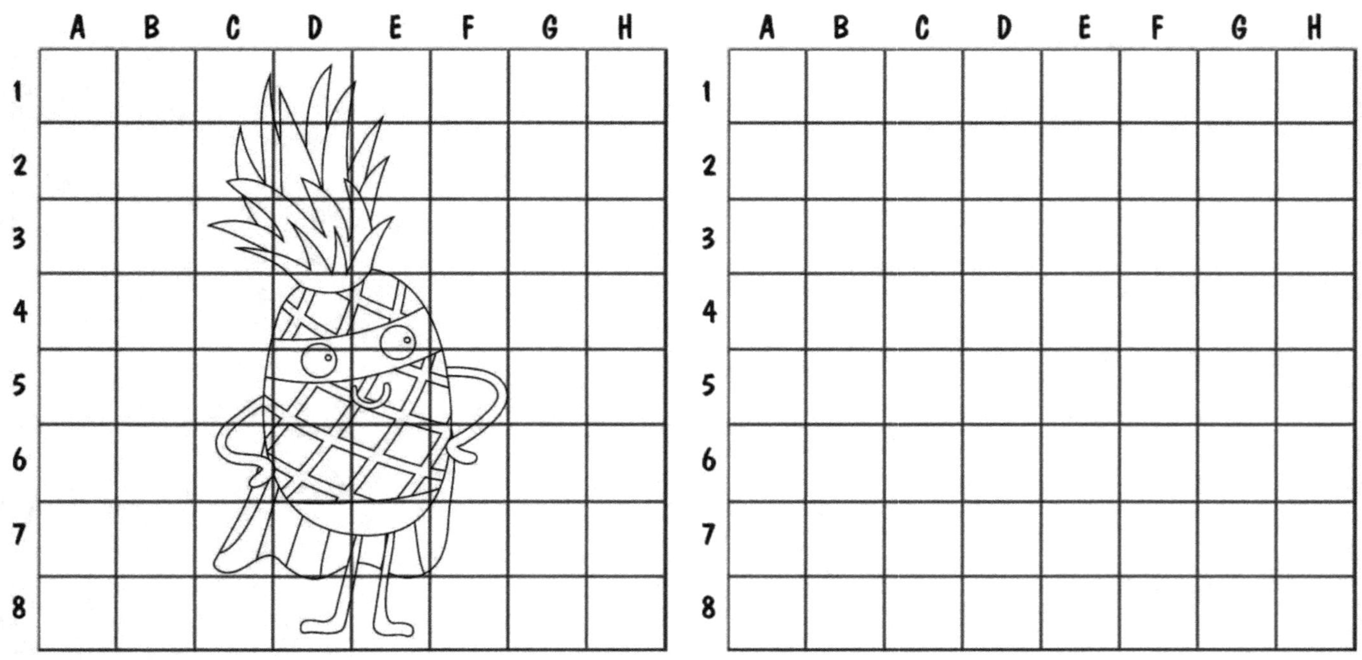

NOW COLOR IT

YOUR TURN TO DRAW

SUPER POMEGRANATE

Step by Step Instructions

Draw inside the box with the help of art grids.

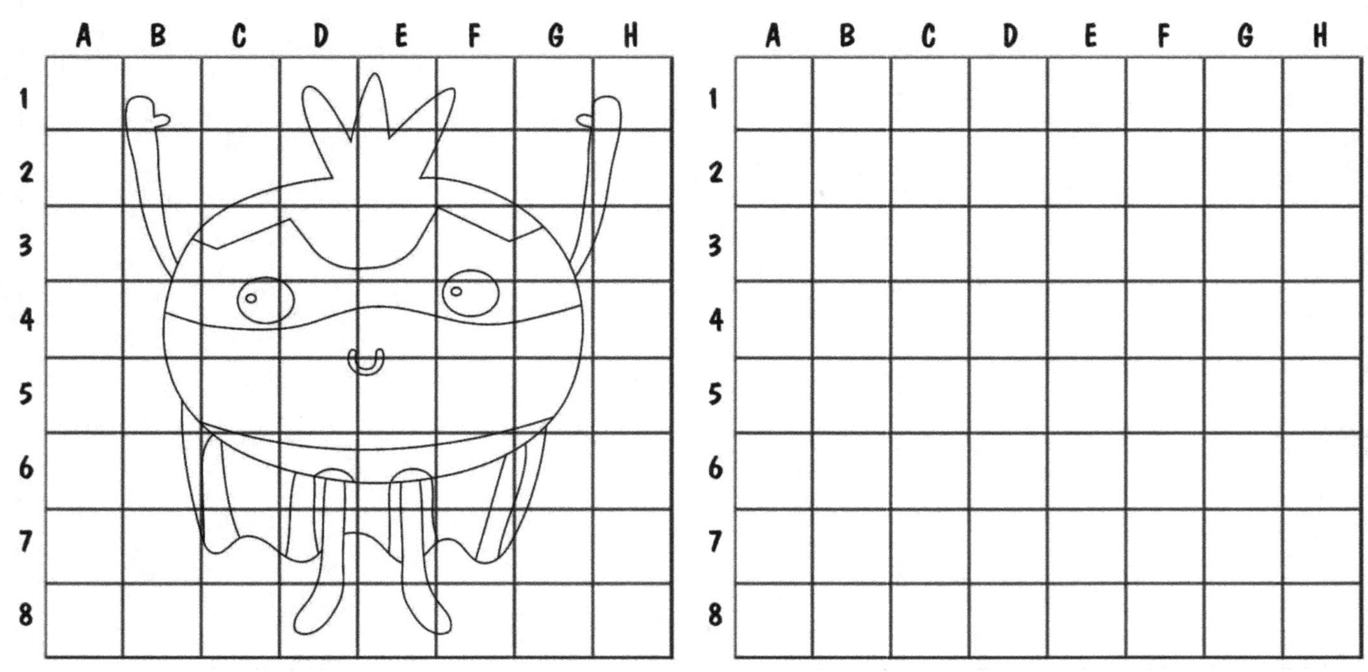

NOW COLOR IT

YOUR TURN TO DRAW

SUPER STRAWBERRY

Step by Step Instructions

Draw inside the box with the help of art grids.

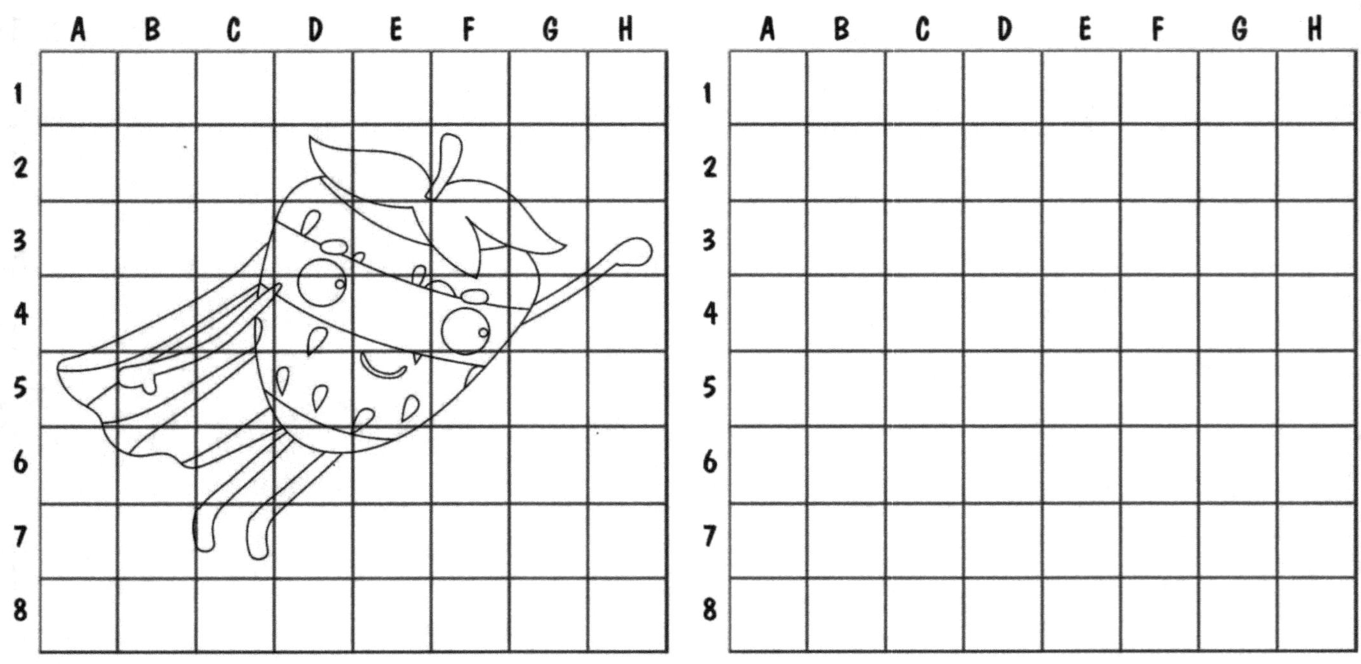

NOW COLOR IT

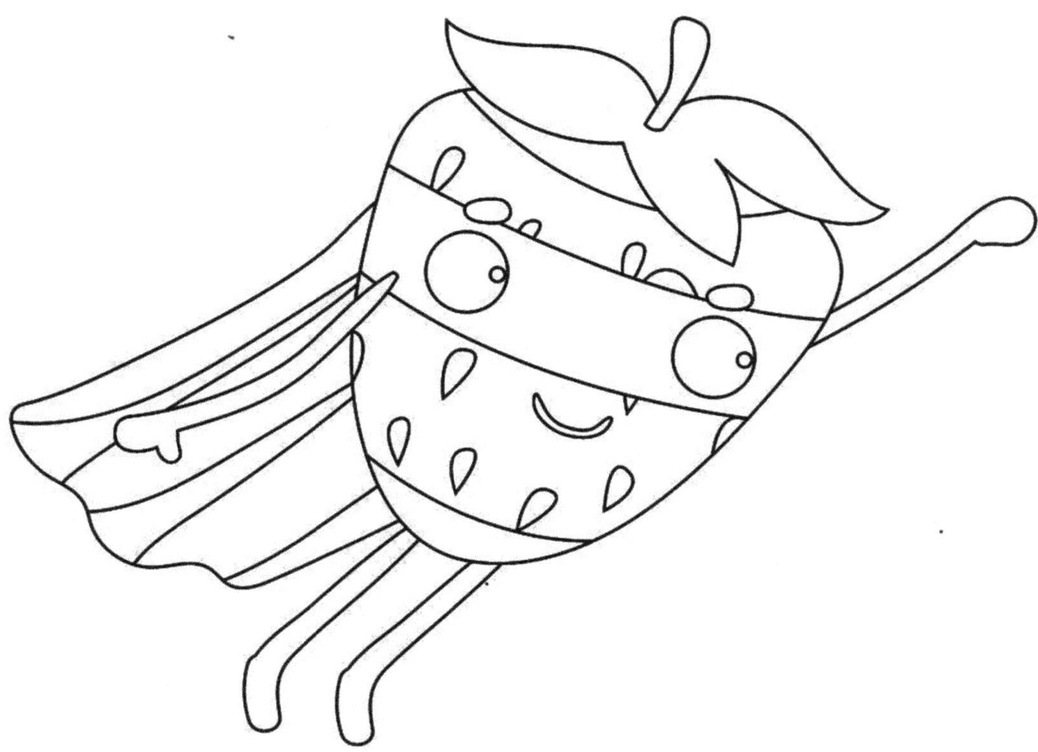

YOUR TURN TO DRAW

SUPER WATERMELON

Step by Step Instructions

Draw inside the box with the help of art grids.

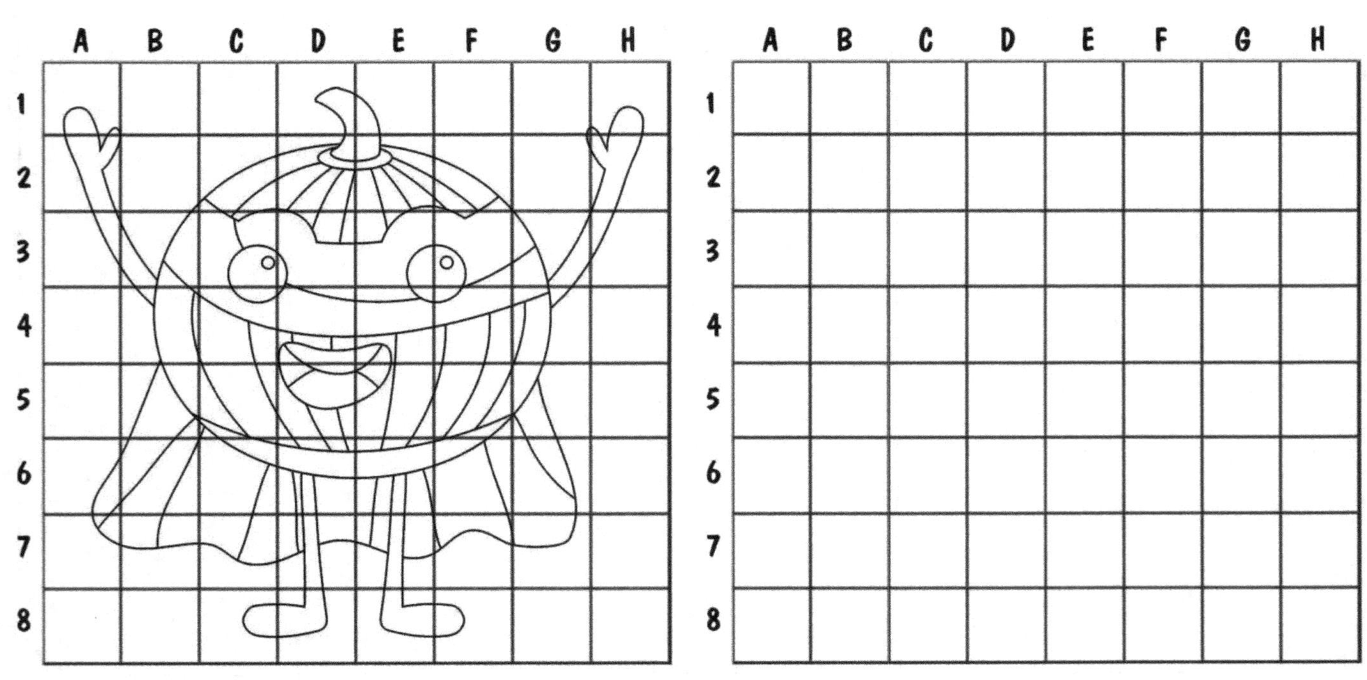

NOW COLOR IT

YOUR TURN TO DRAW

SUPER APPLE
Step by Step Instructions

Draw inside the box with the help of art grids.

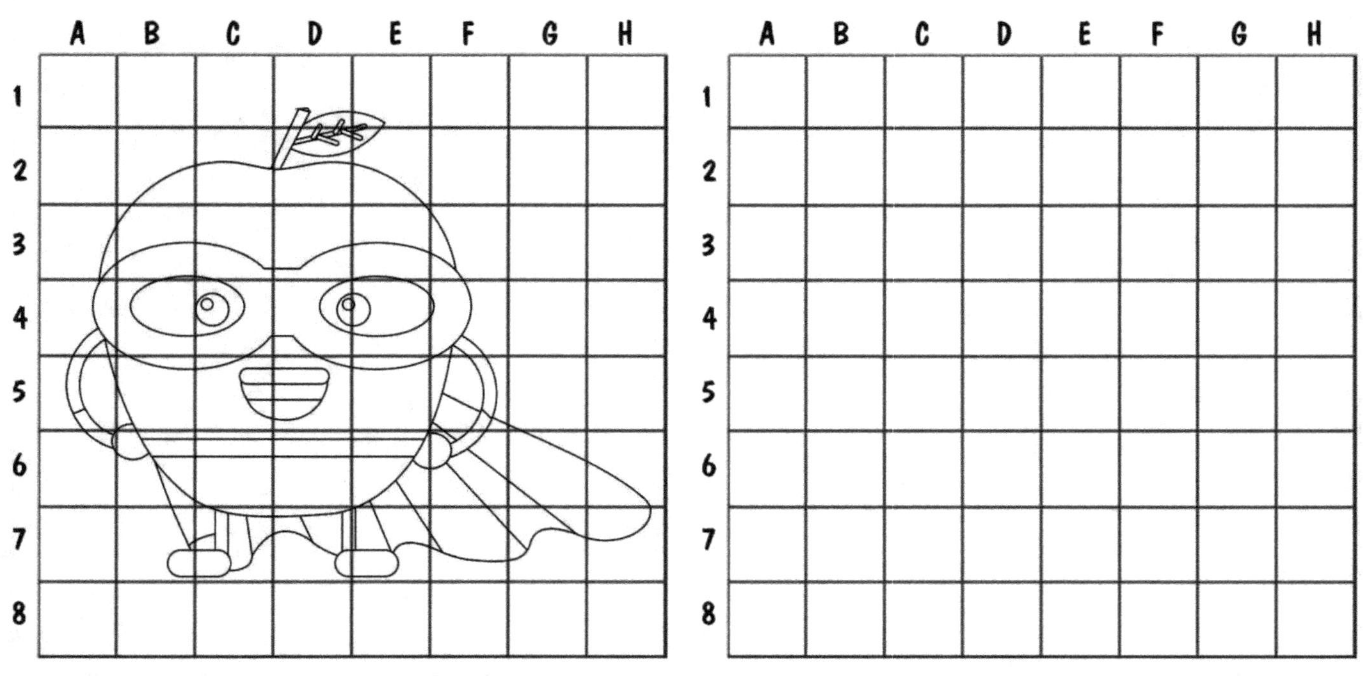

NOW COLOR IT

YOUR TURN TO DRAW

SUPER CHERRY

Step by Step Instructions

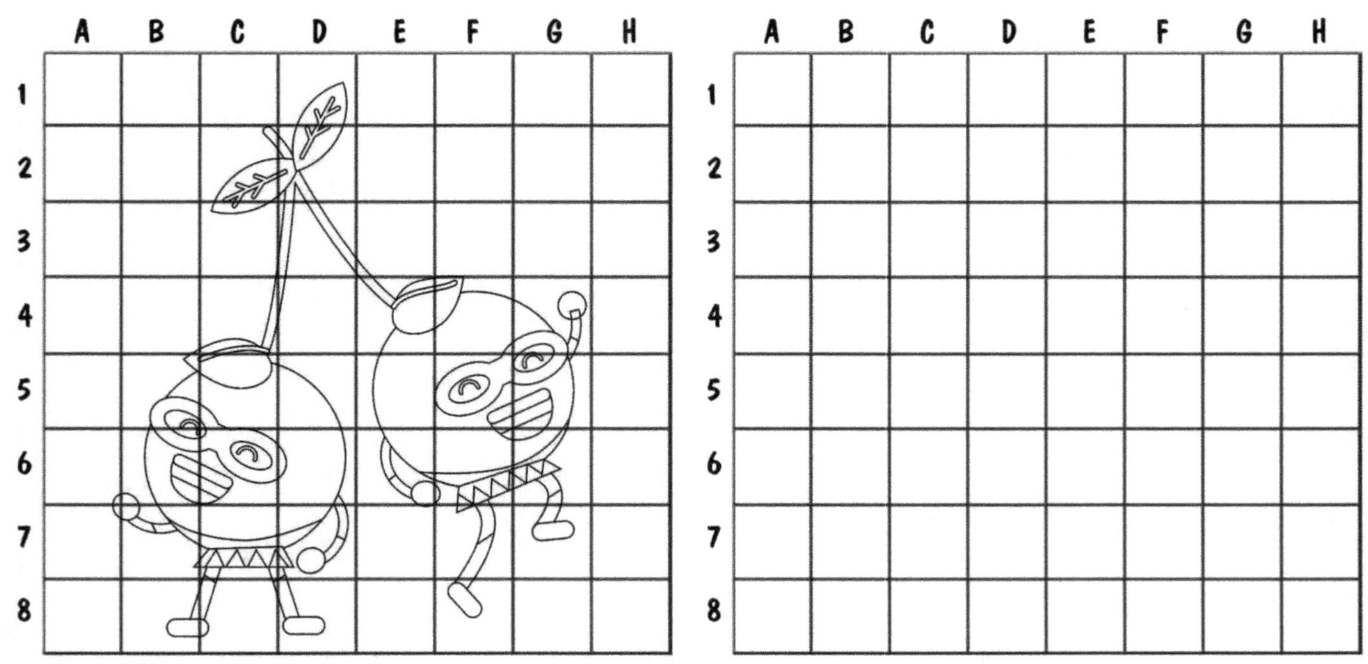

Draw inside the box with the help of art grids.

NOW COLOR IT

YOUR TURN TO DRAW

SUPER GREEN APPLE

Step by Step Instructions

Draw inside the box with the help of art grids.

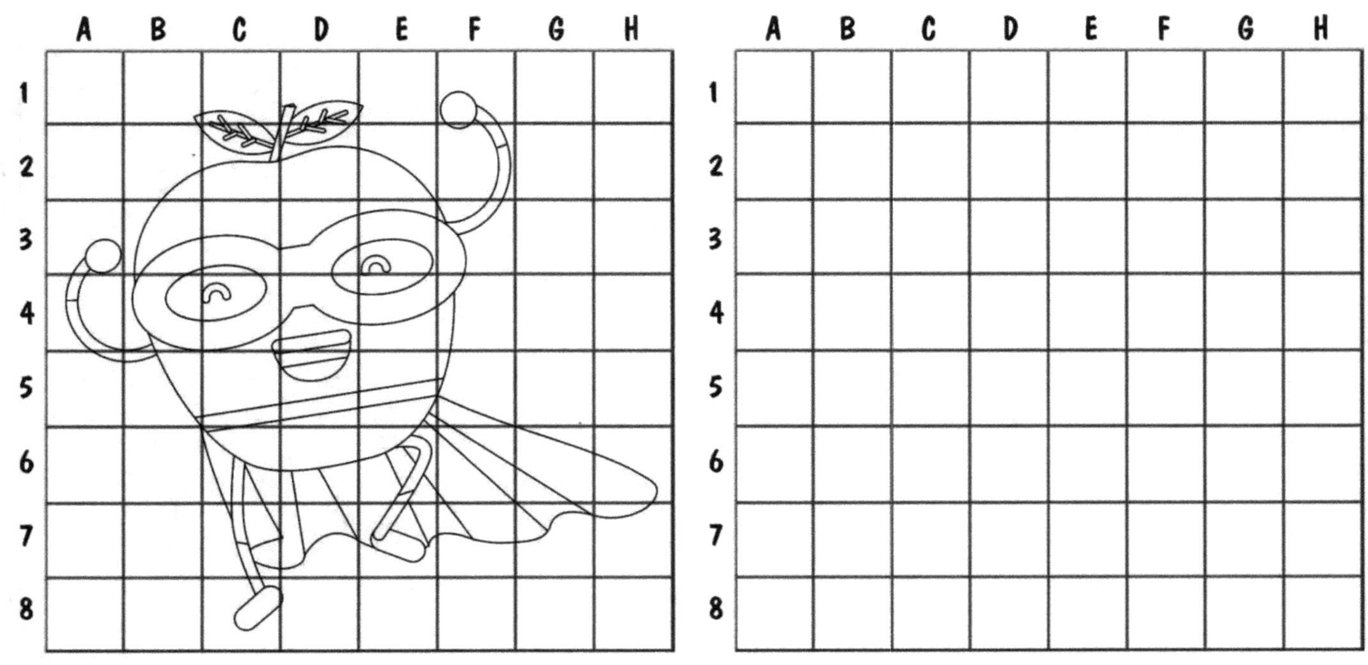

NOW COLOR IT

YOUR TURN TO DRAW

SUPER LEMON

Step by Step Instructions

Draw inside the box with the help of art grids.

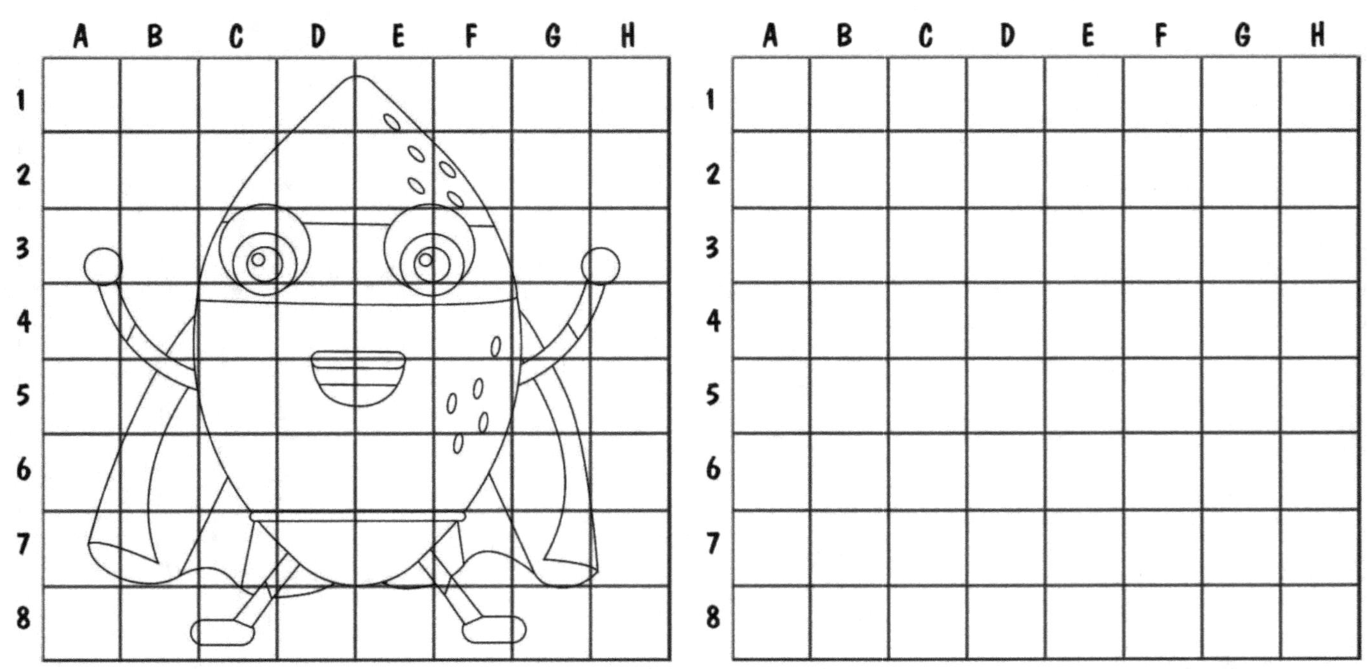

NOW COLOR IT

YOUR TURN TO DRAW

SUPER ORANGE

Step by Step Instructions

Draw inside the box with the help of art grids.

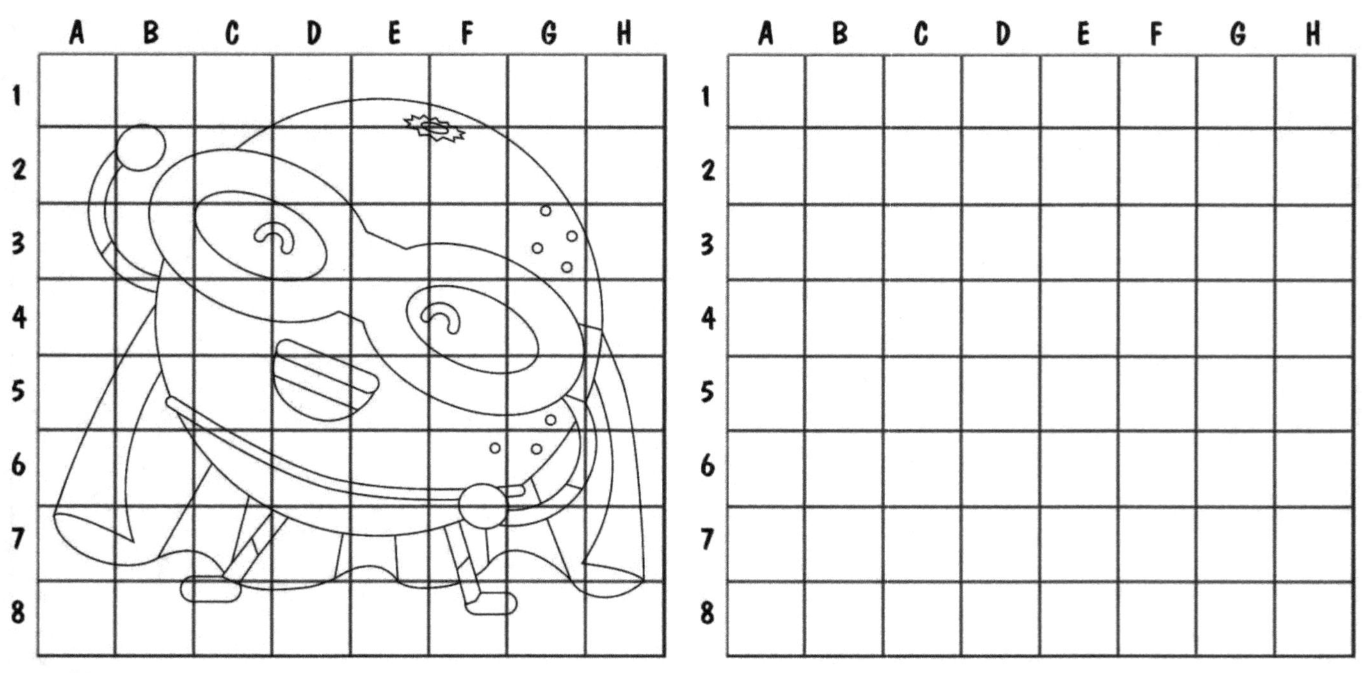

NOW COLOR IT

YOUR TURN TO DRAW

SUPER PEAR
Step by Step Instructions

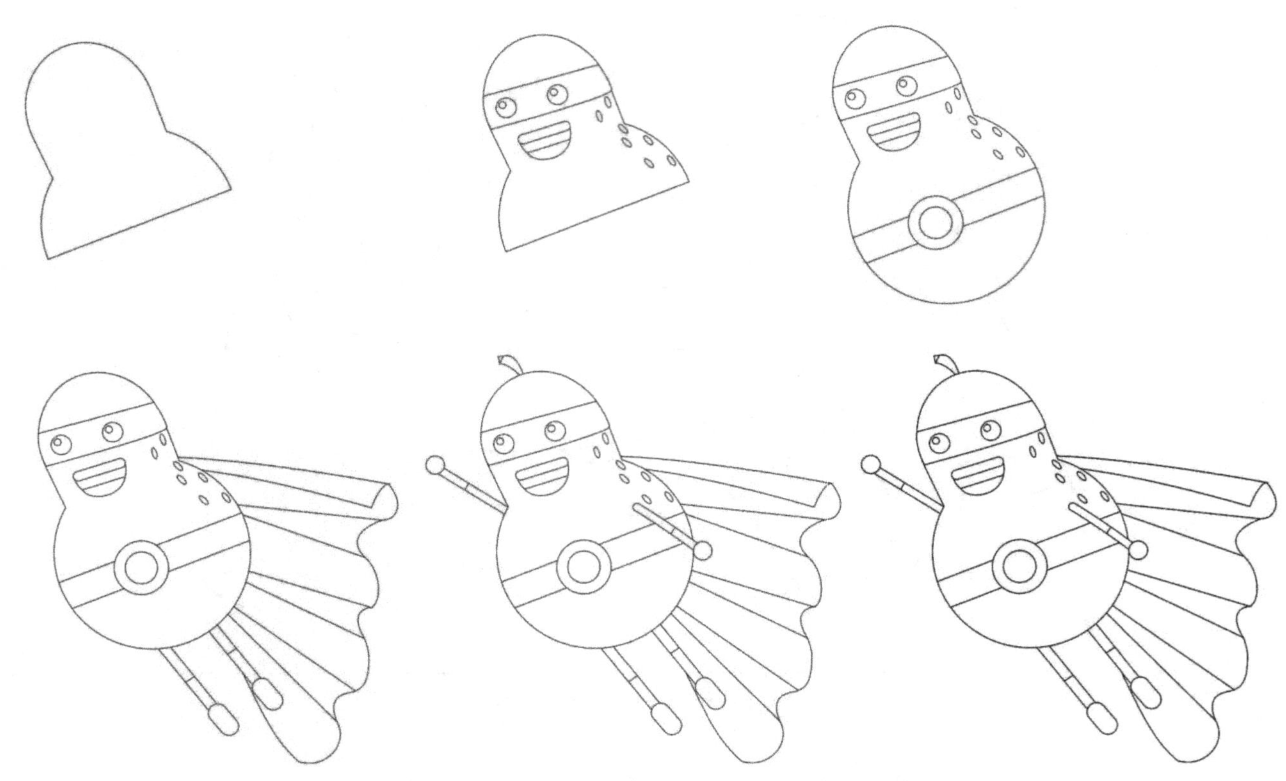

Draw inside the box with the help of art grids.

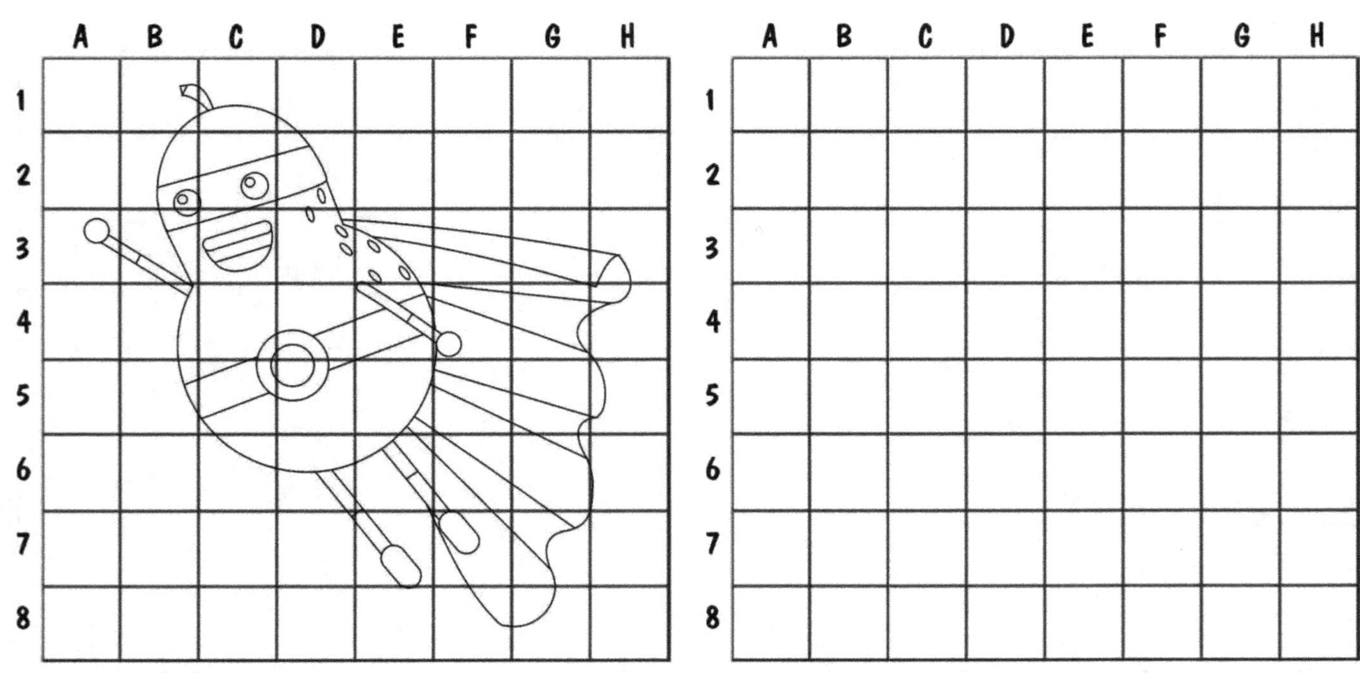

NOW COLOR IT

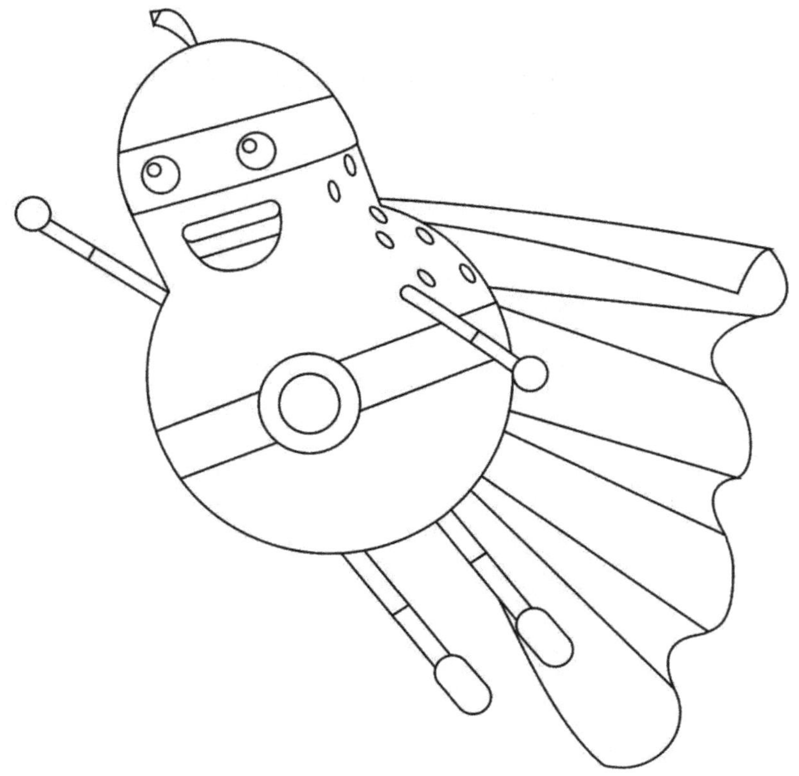

YOUR TURN TO DRAW

SUPER PINEAPPLE

Step by Step Instructions

Draw inside the box with the help of art grids.

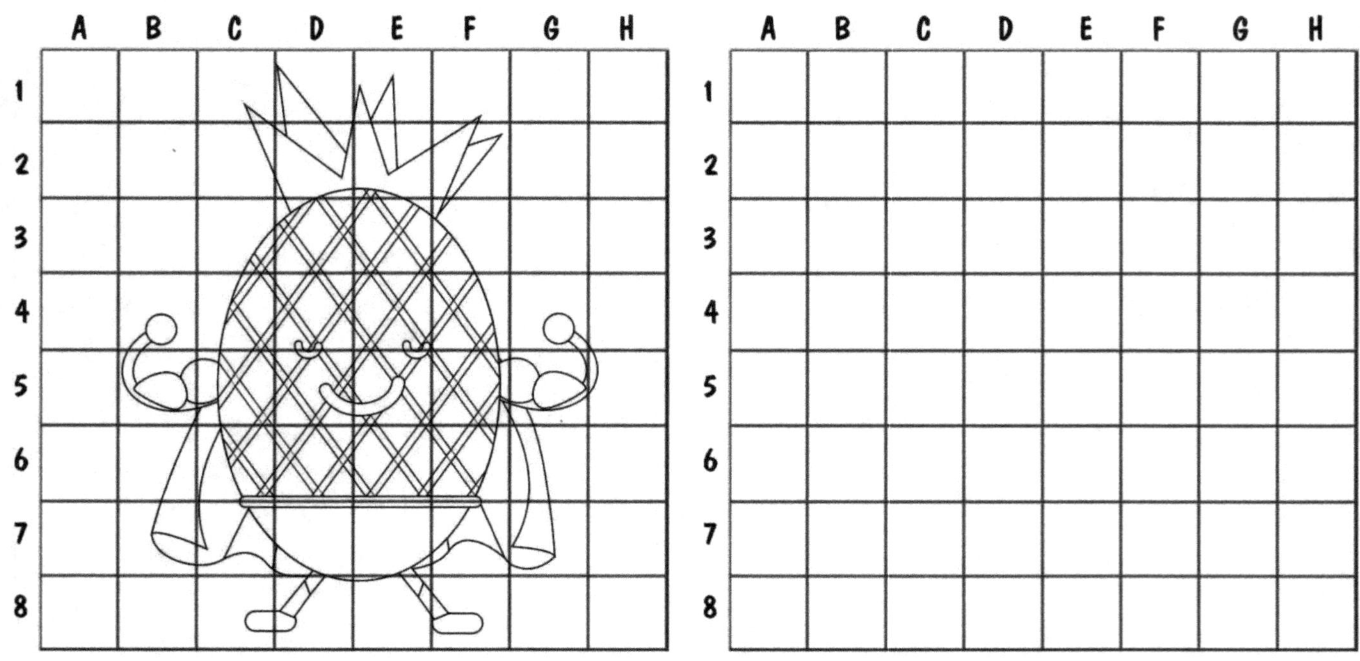

NOW COLOR IT

YOUR TURN TO DRAW

SUPER PLUM

Step by Step Instructions

Draw inside the box with the help of art grids.

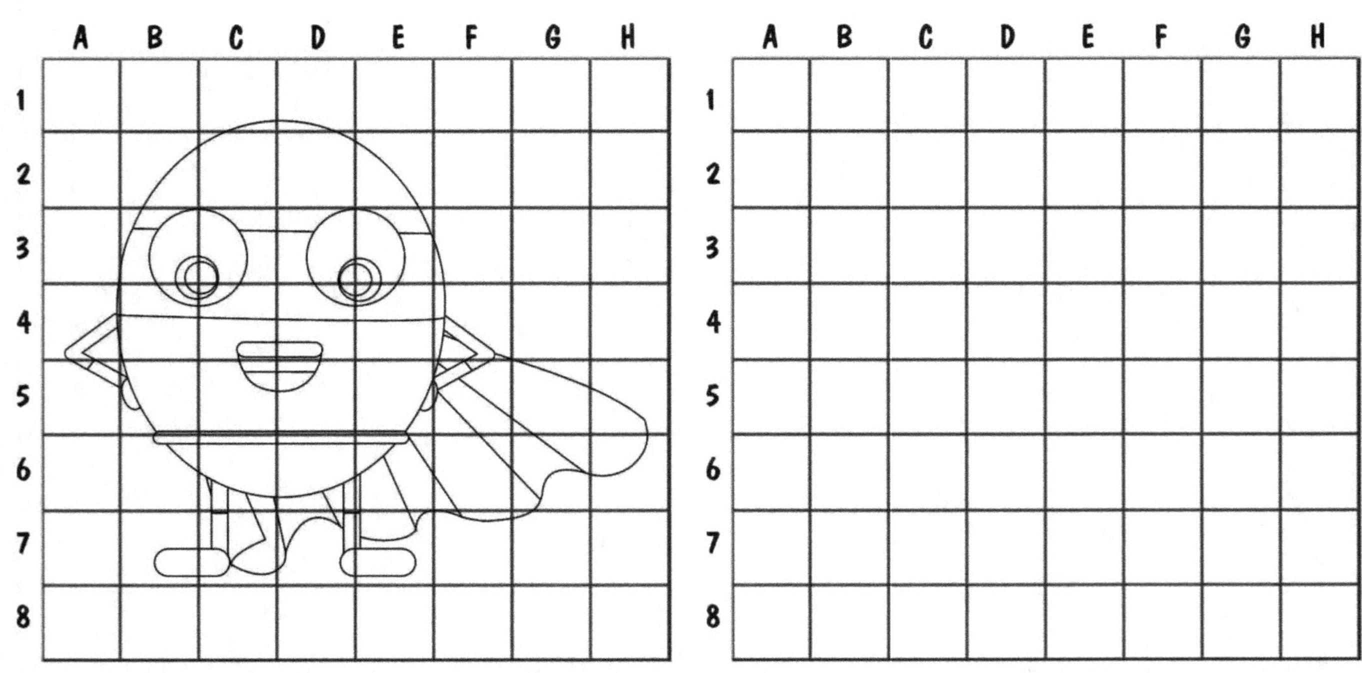

NOW COLOR IT

YOUR TURN TO DRAW

SUPER STRAWBERRY

Step by Step Instructions

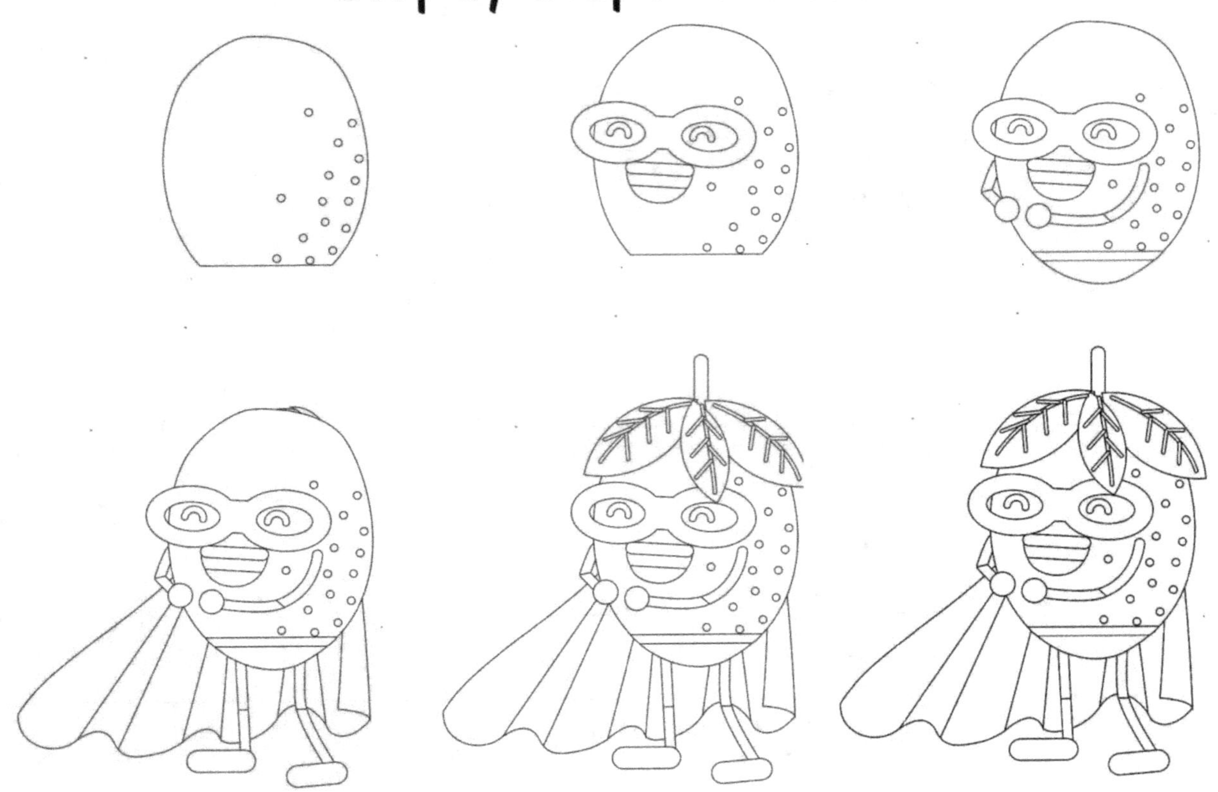

Draw inside the box with the help of art grids.

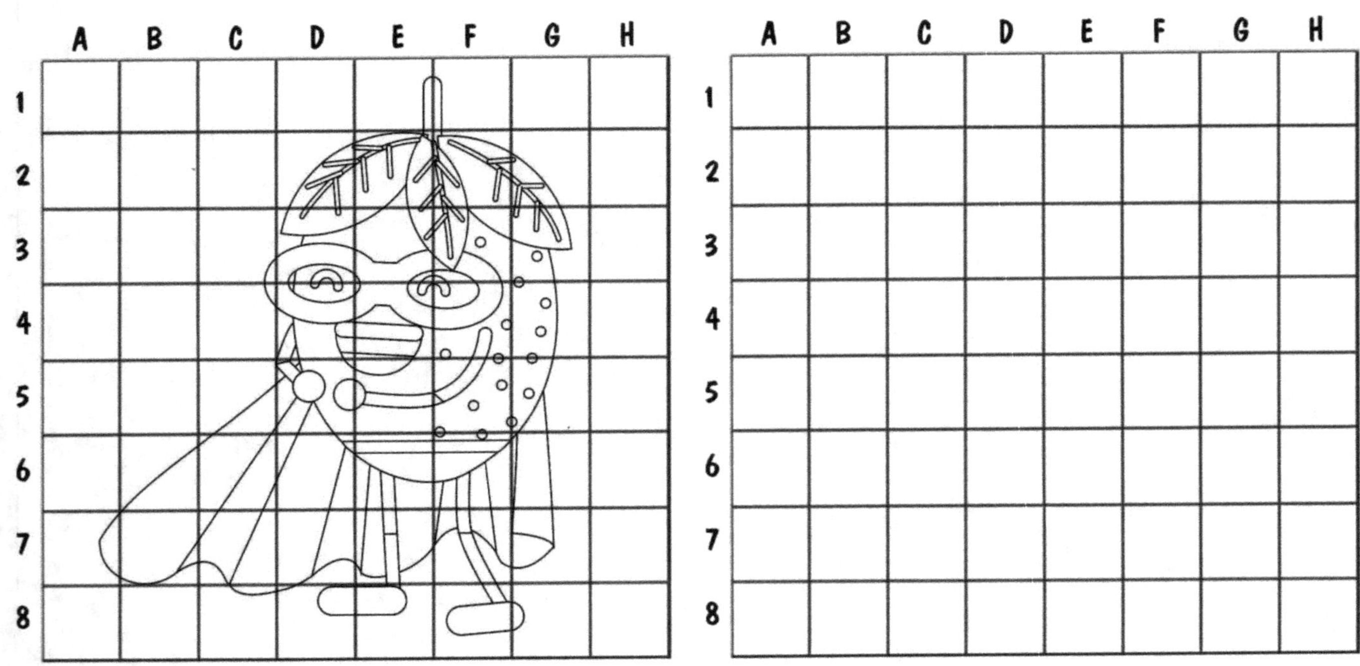

NOW COLOR IT

YOUR TURN TO DRAW

SUPER BRINJAL

Step by Step Instructions

Draw inside the box with the help of art grids.

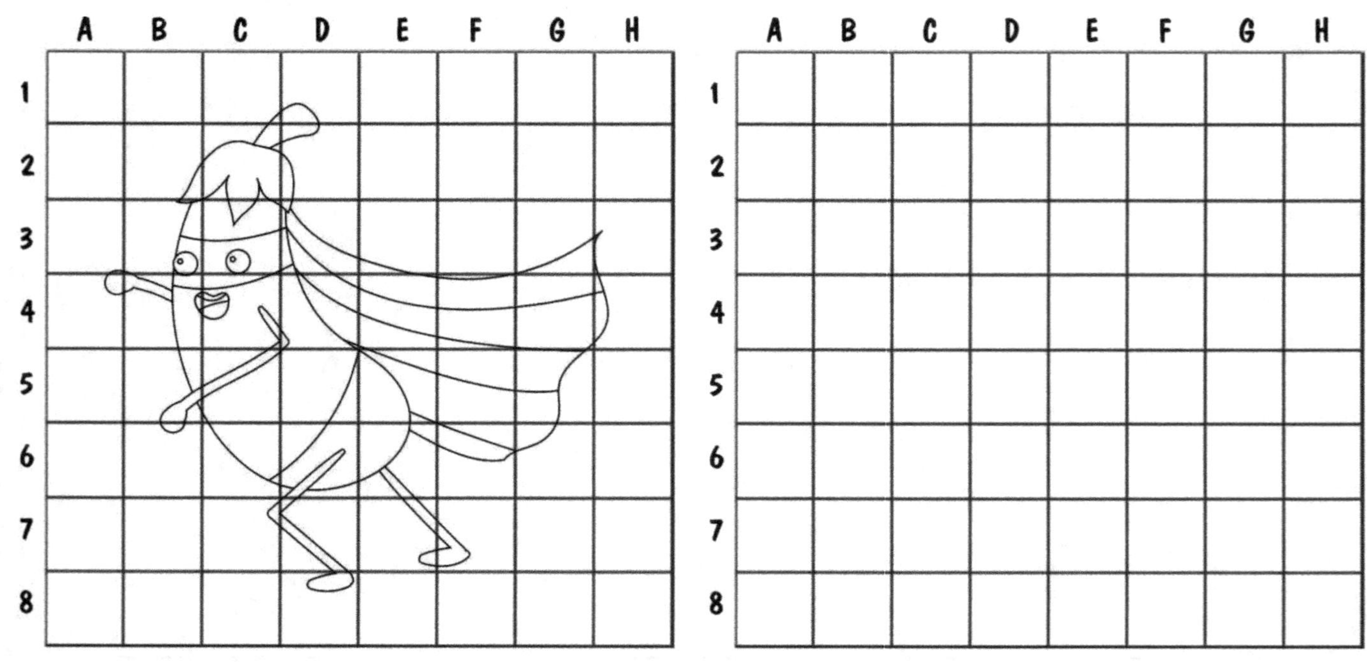

NOW COLOR IT

YOUR TURN TO DRAW

SUPER BROCCOLI

Step by Step Instructions

Draw inside the box with the help of art grids.

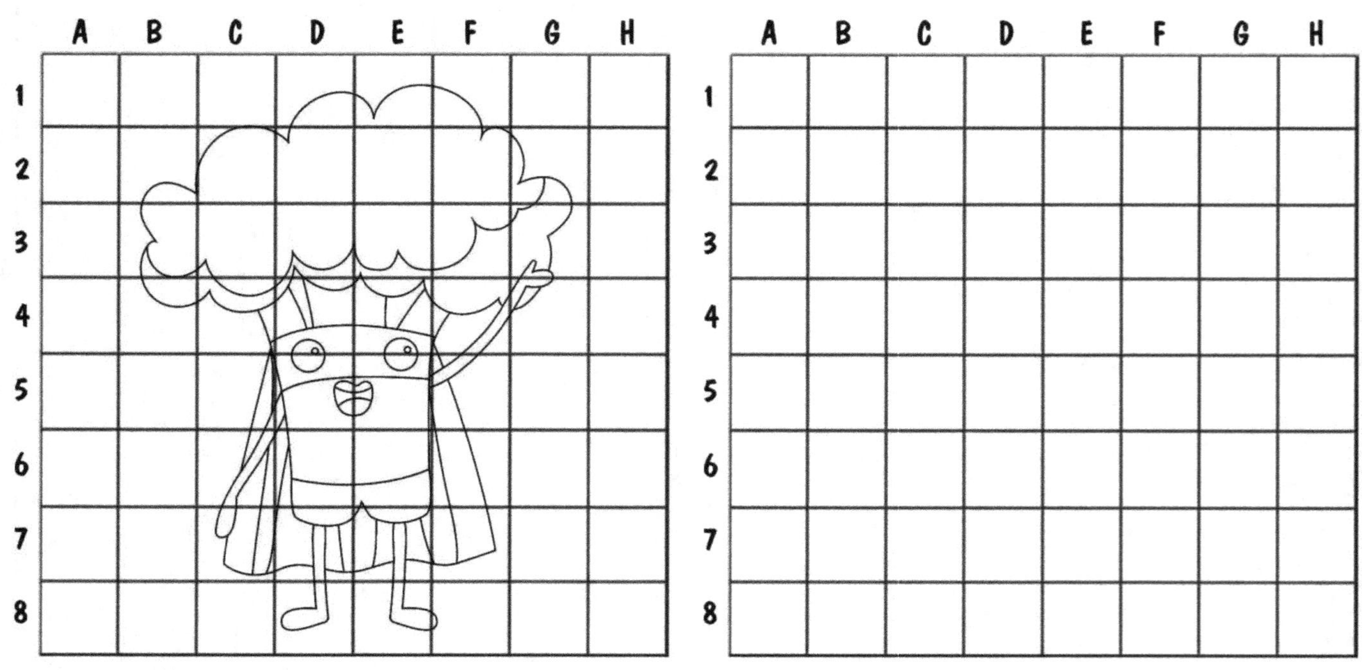

NOW COLOR IT

YOUR TURN TO DRAW

SUPER CAPSICUM

Step by Step Instructions

Draw inside the box with the help of art grids.

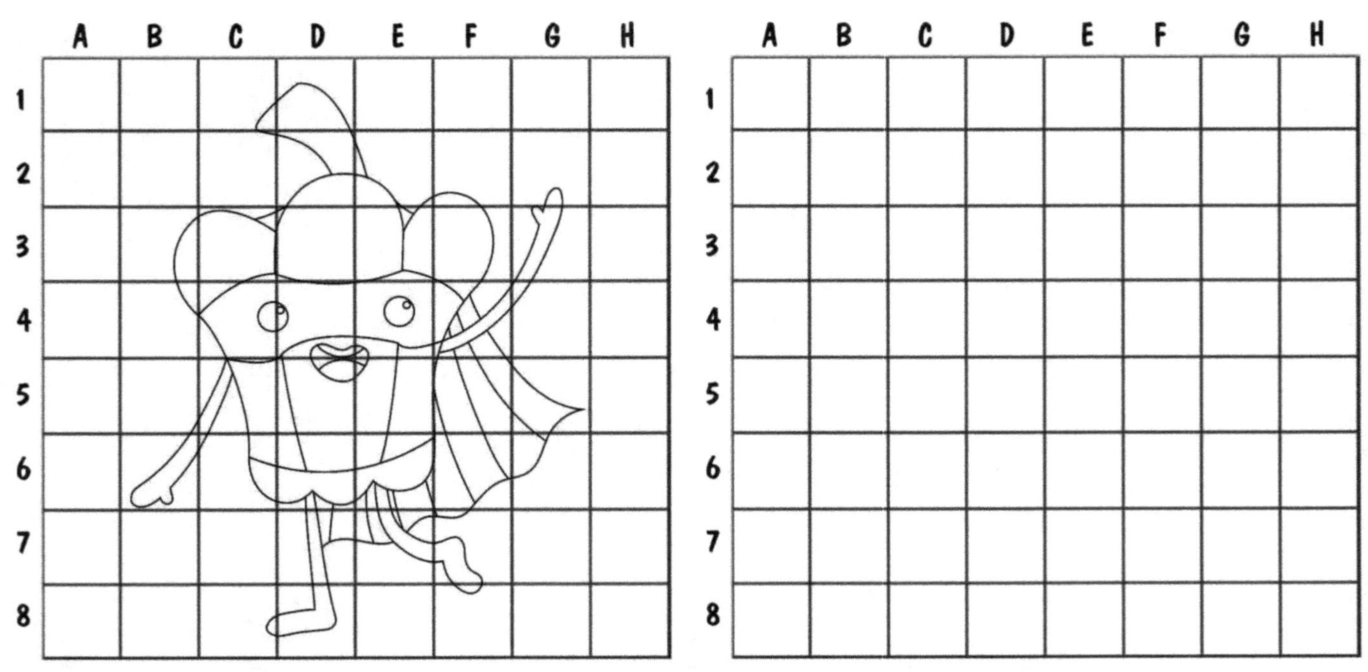

NOW COLOR IT

YOUR TURN TO DRAW

SUPER CARROT

Step by Step Instructions

Draw inside the box with the help of art grids.

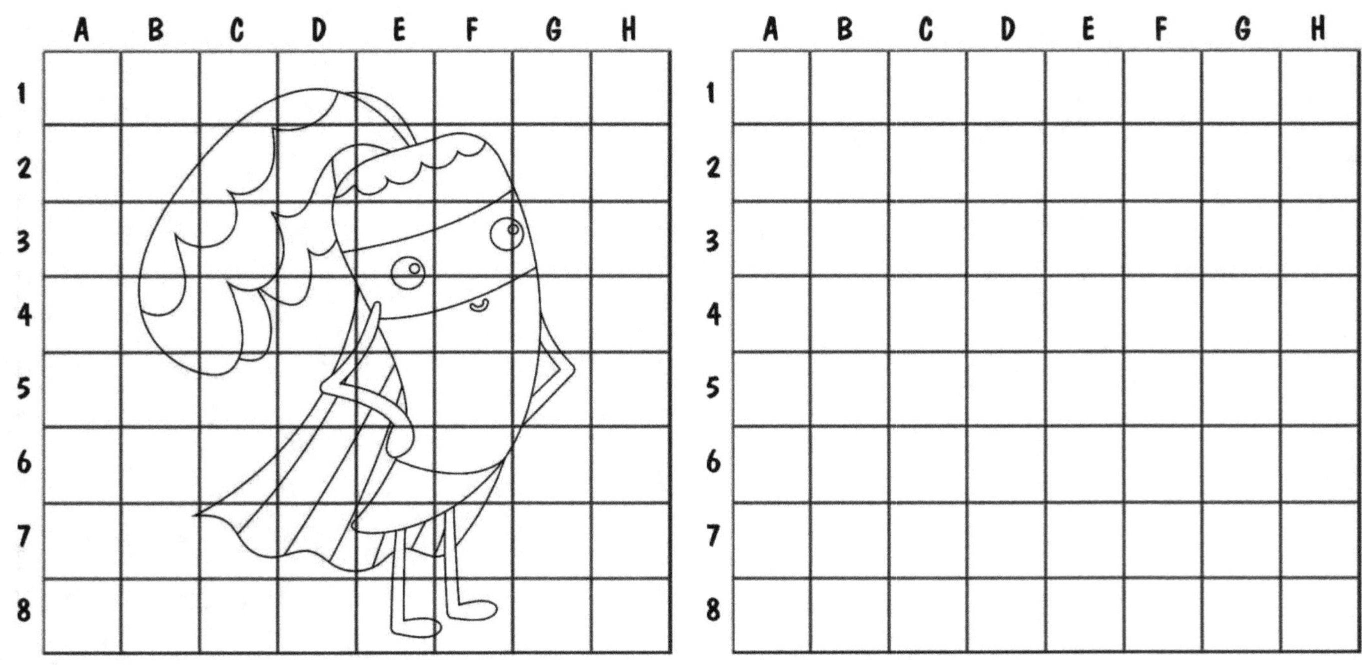

NOW COLOR IT

YOUR TURN TO DRAW

SUPER GREEN ONION

Step by Step Instructions

Draw inside the box with the help of art grids.

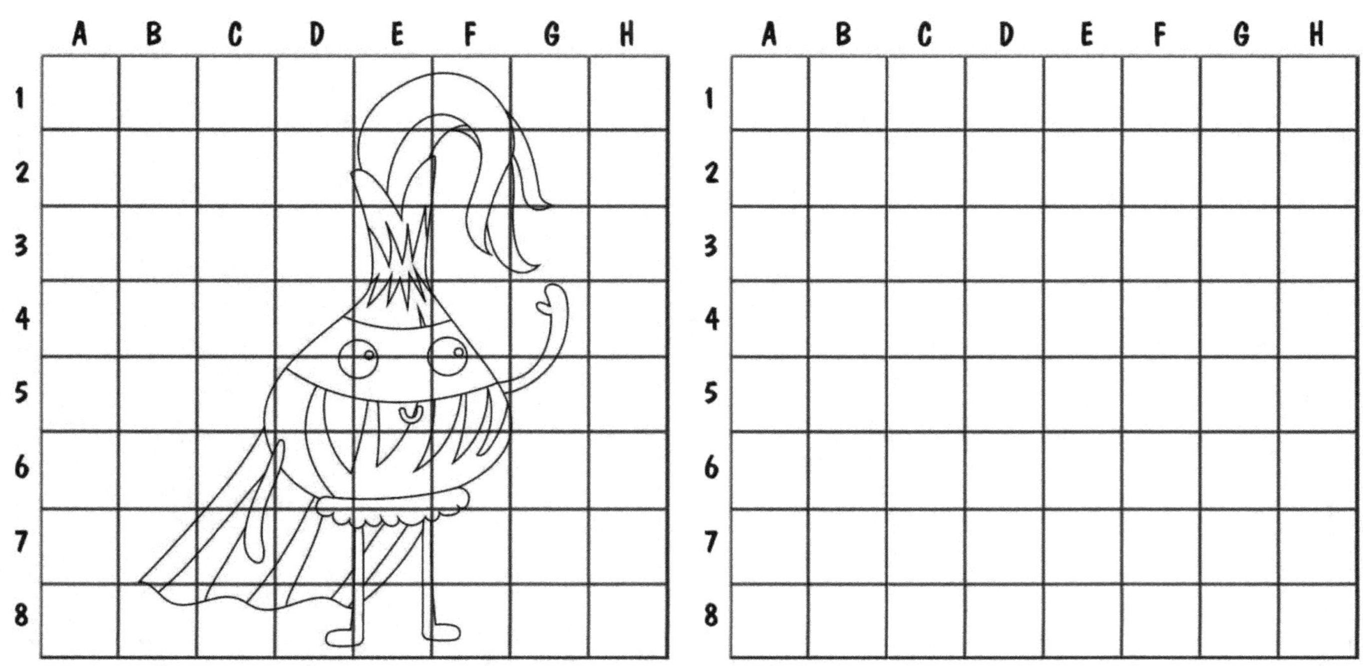

NOW COLOR IT

YOUR TURN TO DRAW

SUPER PATTYPAN

Step by Step Instructions

Draw inside the box with the help of art grids.

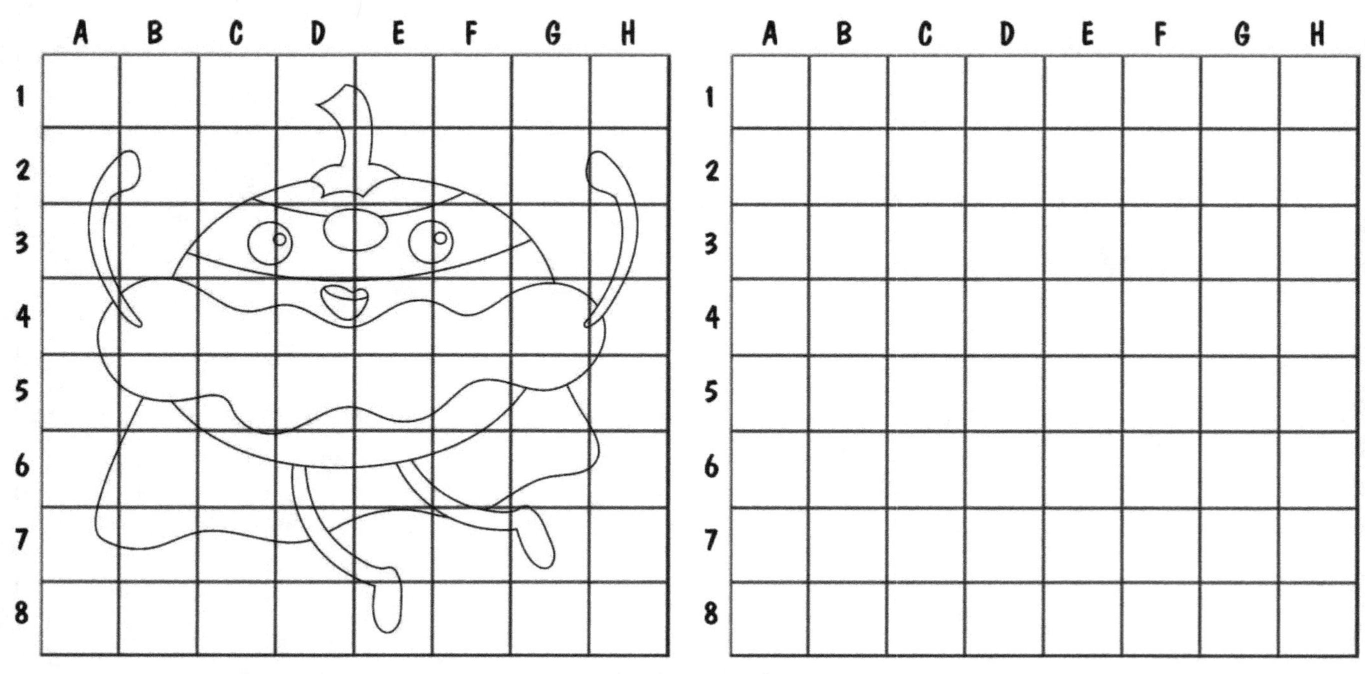

NOW COLOR IT

YOUR TURN TO DRAW

SUPER POTATO

Step by Step Instructions

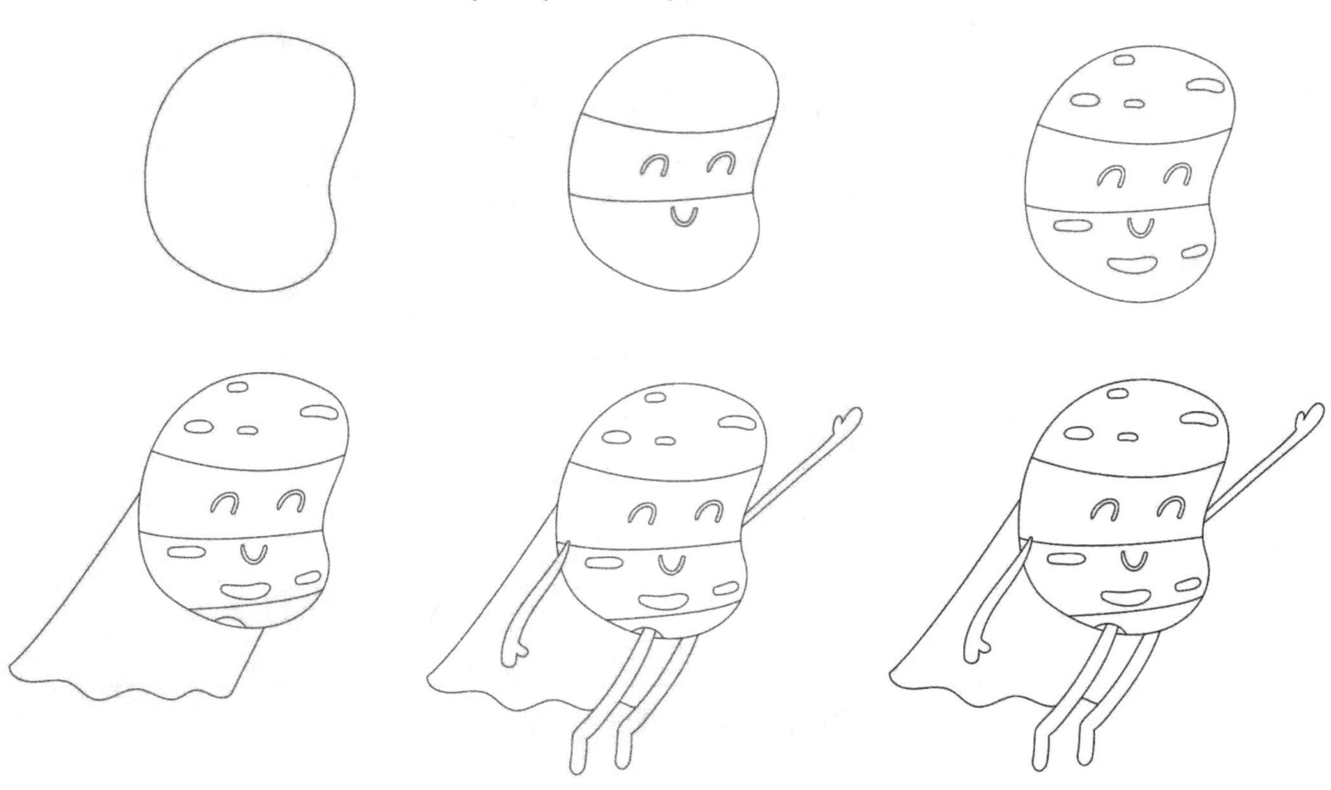

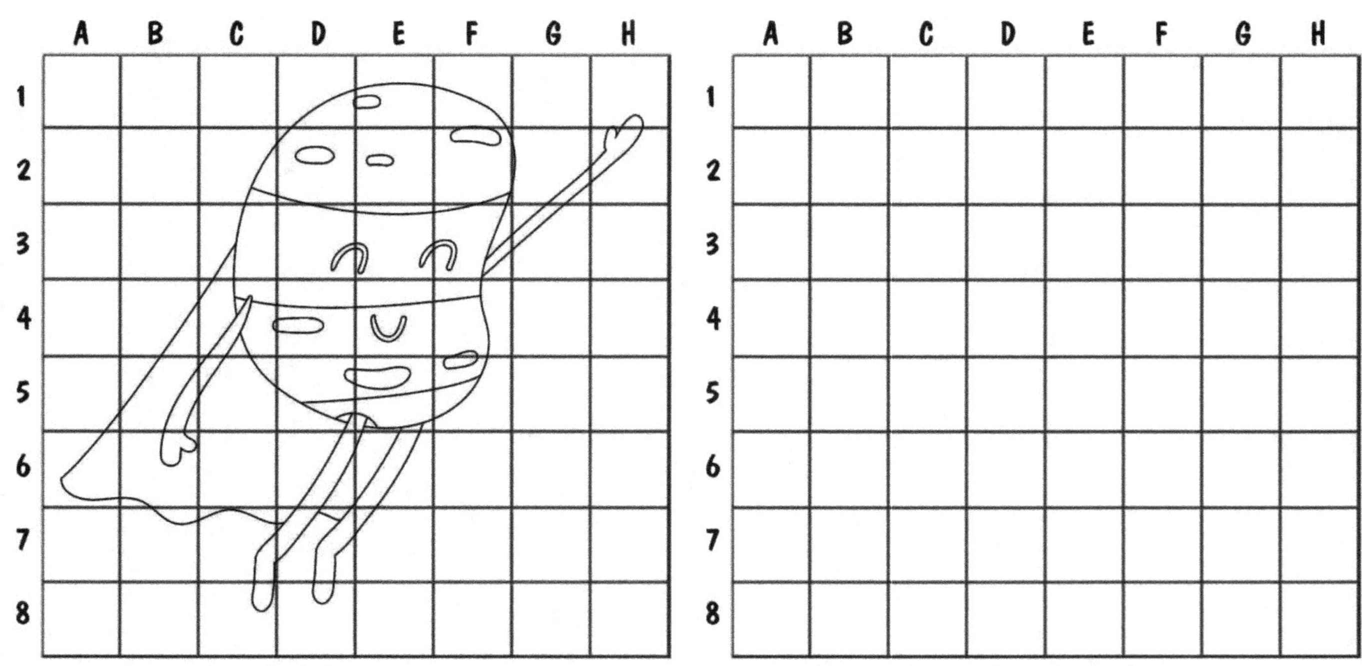

Draw inside the box with the help of art grids.

NOW COLOR IT

YOUR TURN TO DRAW

SUPER PUMPKIN

Step by Step Instructions

Draw inside the box with the help of art grids.

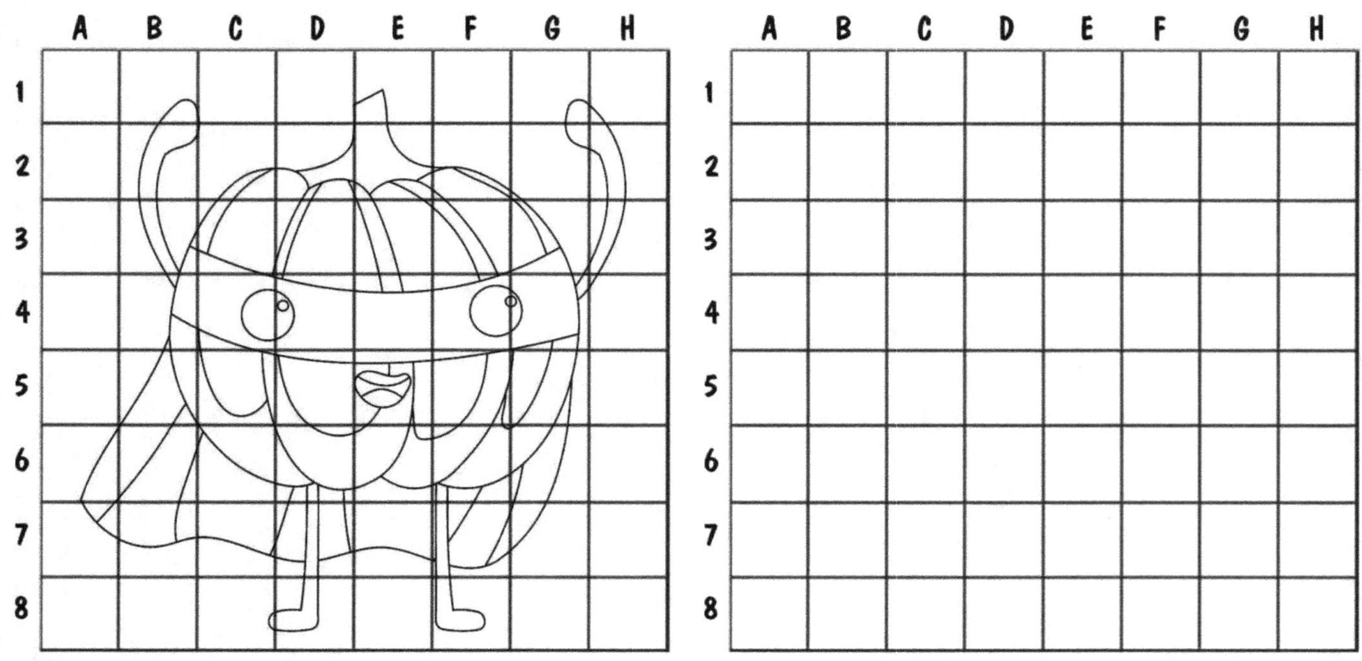

NOW COLOR IT

YOUR TURN TO DRAW

SUPER TOMATO

Step by Step Instructions

Draw inside the box with the help of art grids.

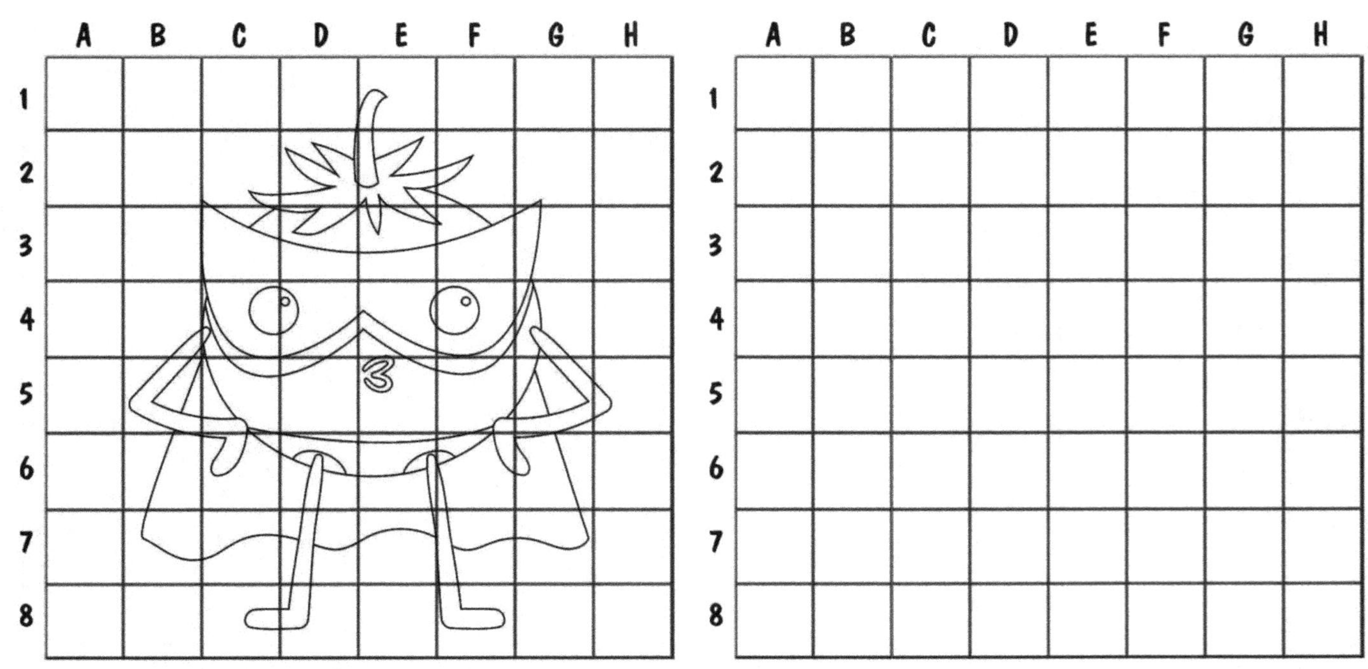

NOW COLOR IT

YOUR TURN TO DRAW

SUPER BRINJAL

Step by Step Instructions

Draw inside the box with the help of art grids.

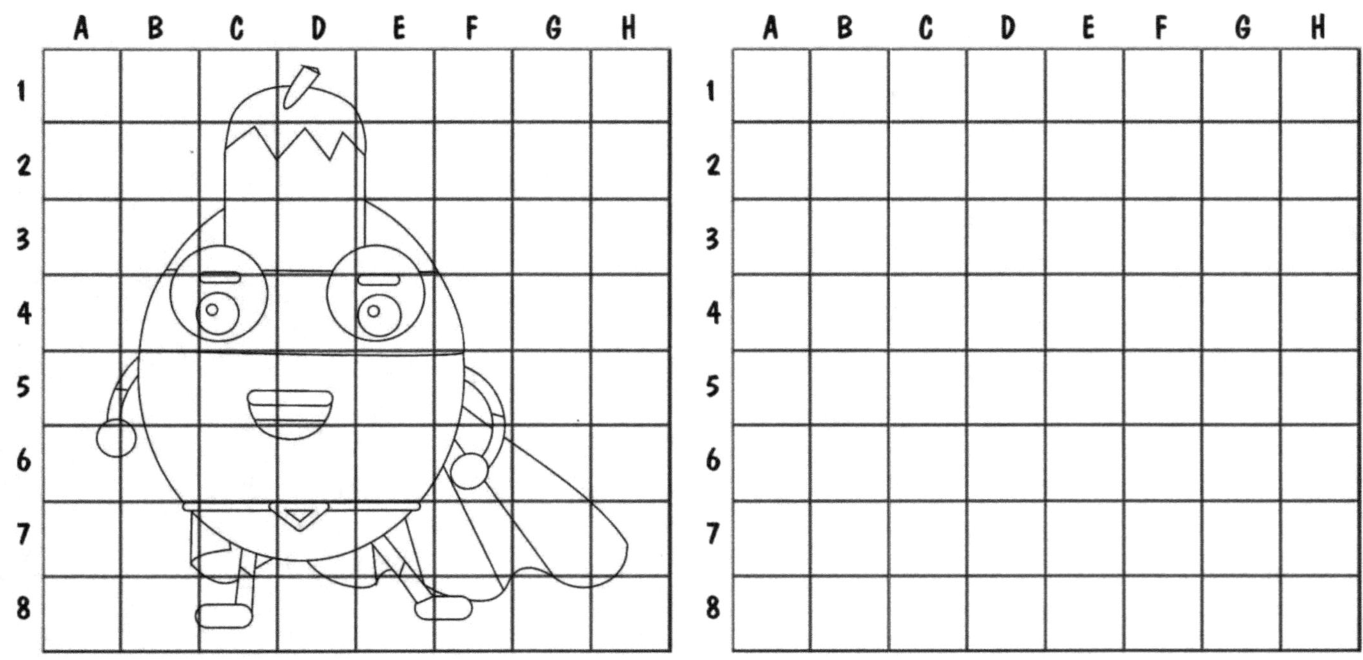

NOW COLOR IT

YOUR TURN TO DRAW

SUPER CABBAGE

Step by Step Instructions

Draw inside the box with the help of art grids.

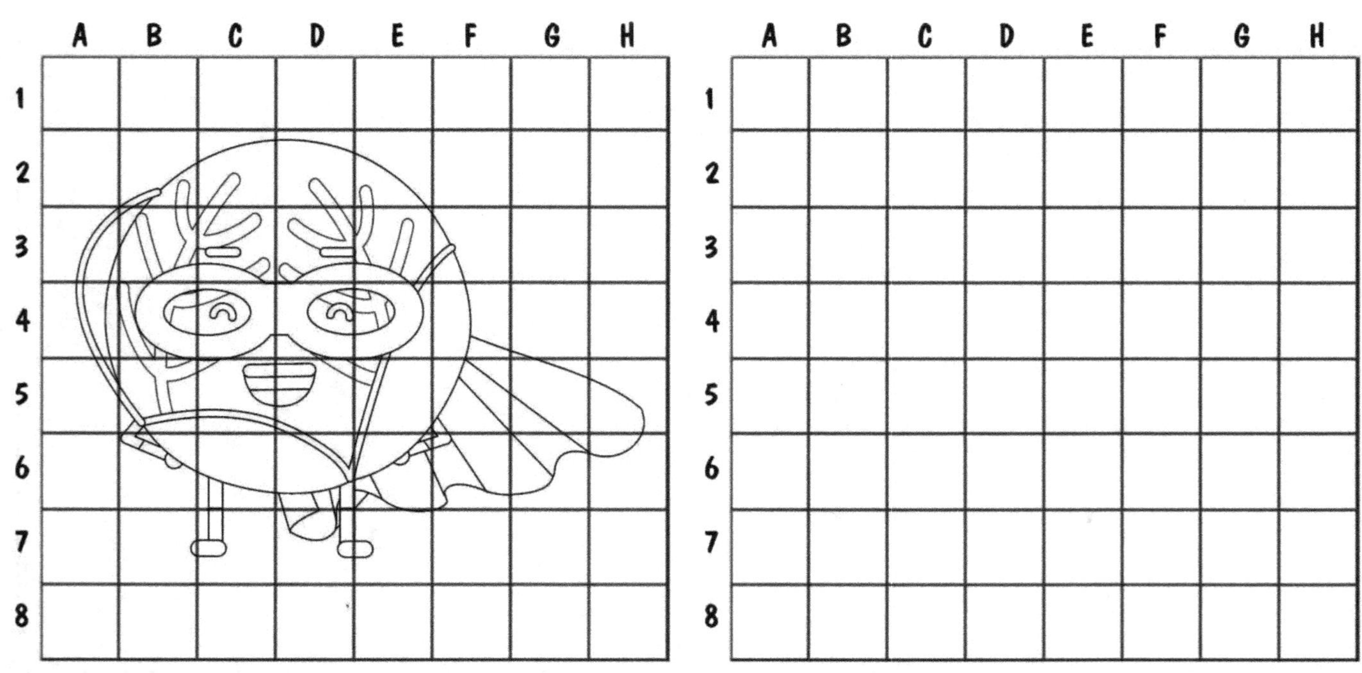

NOW COLOR IT

YOUR TURN TO DRAW

SUPER CAPSICUM

Step by Step Instructions

Draw inside the box with the help of art grids.

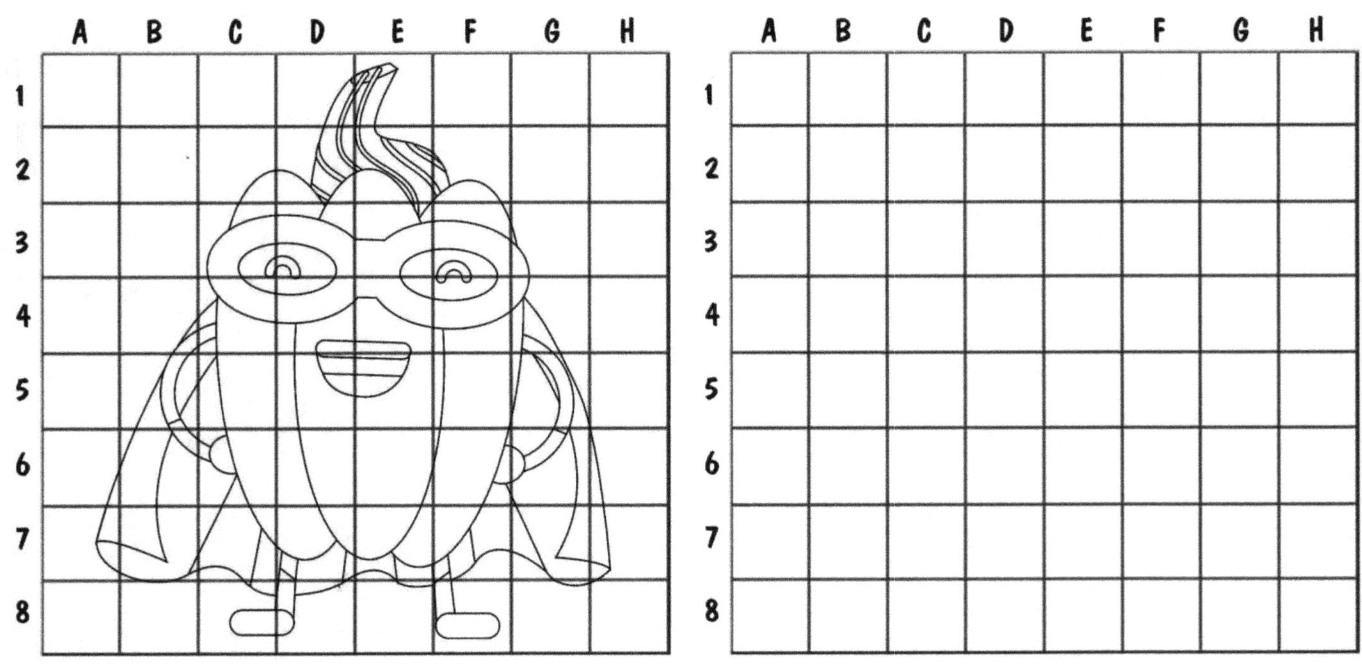

NOW COLOR IT

YOUR TURN TO DRAW

SUPER CARROT

Step by Step Instructions

Draw inside the box with the help of art grids.

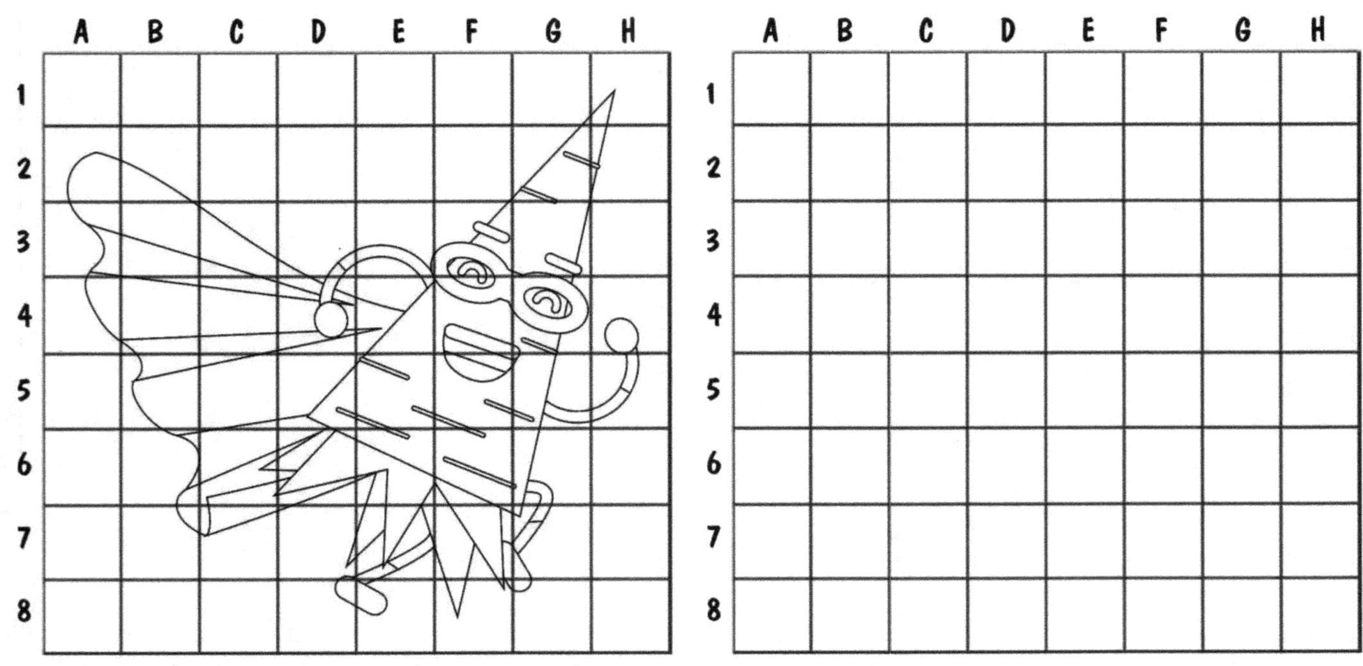

NOW COLOR IT

YOUR TURN TO DRAW

SUPER CORN

Step by Step Instructions

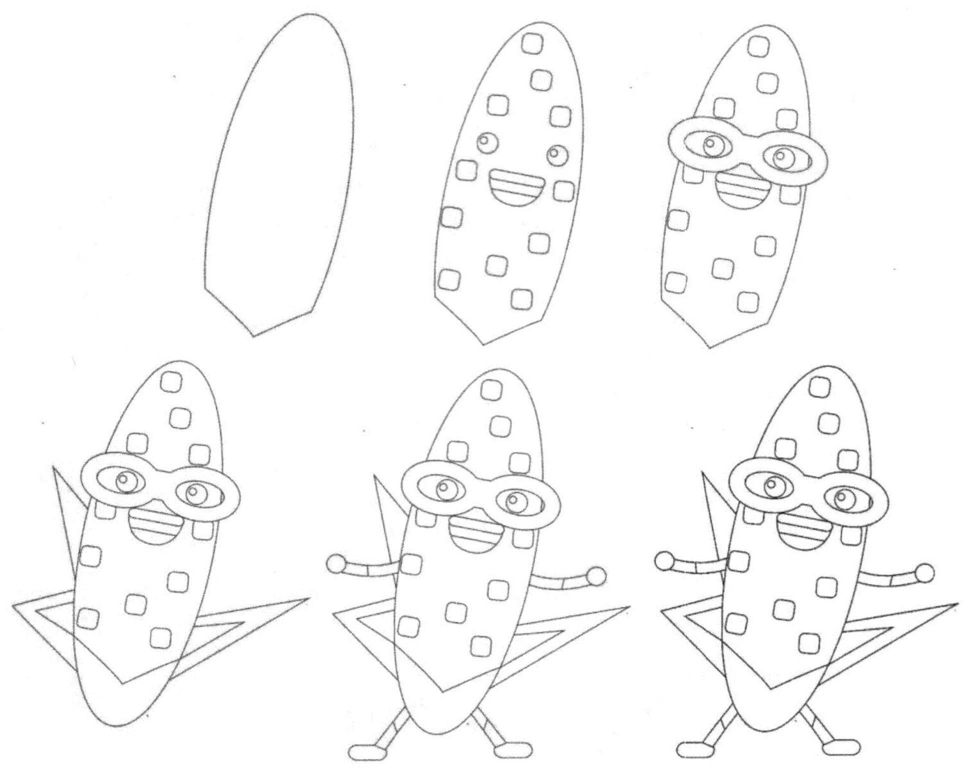

Draw inside the box with the help of art grids.

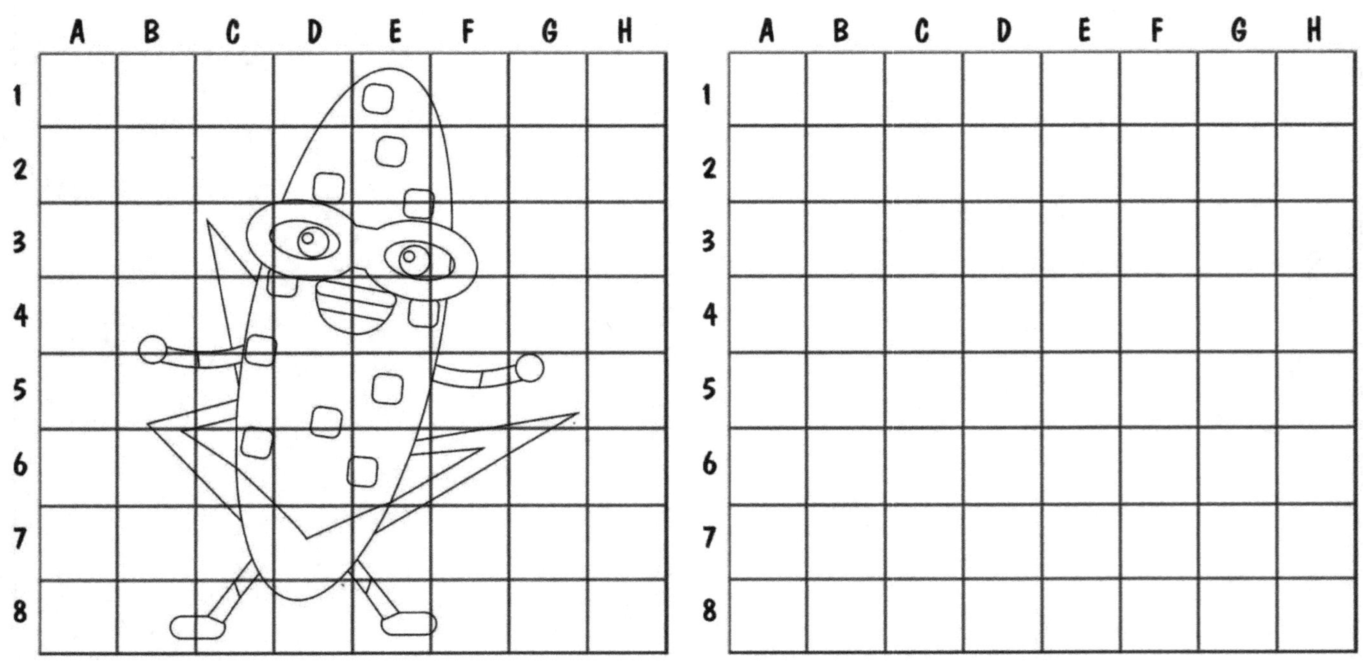

NOW COLOR IT

YOUR TURN TO DRAW

SUPER GARLIC

Step by Step Instructions

Draw inside the box with the help of art grids.

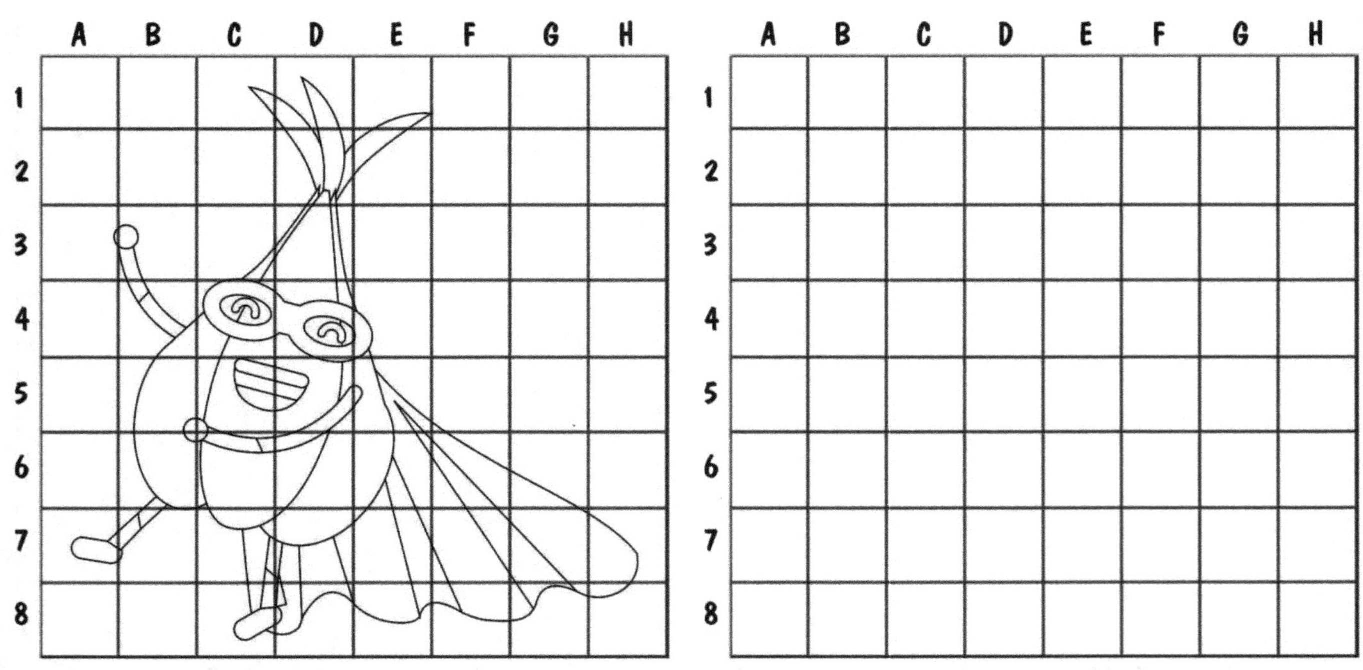

NOW COLOR IT

YOUR TURN TO DRAW

SUPER PUMPKIN

Step by Step Instructions

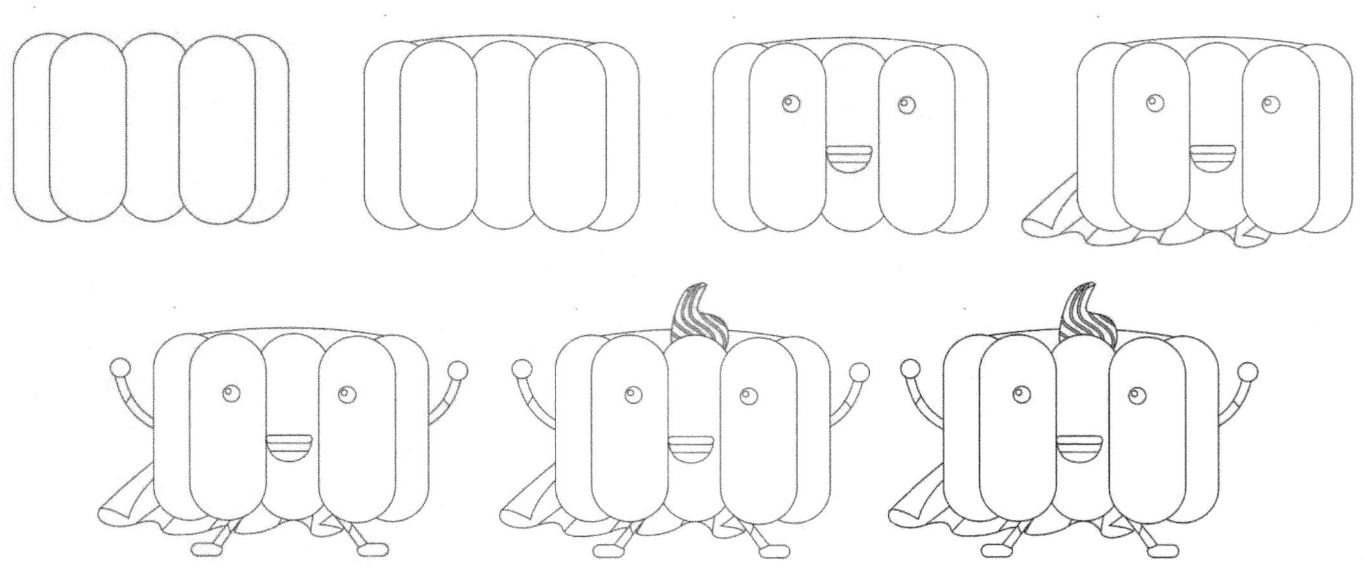

Draw inside the box with the help of art grids.

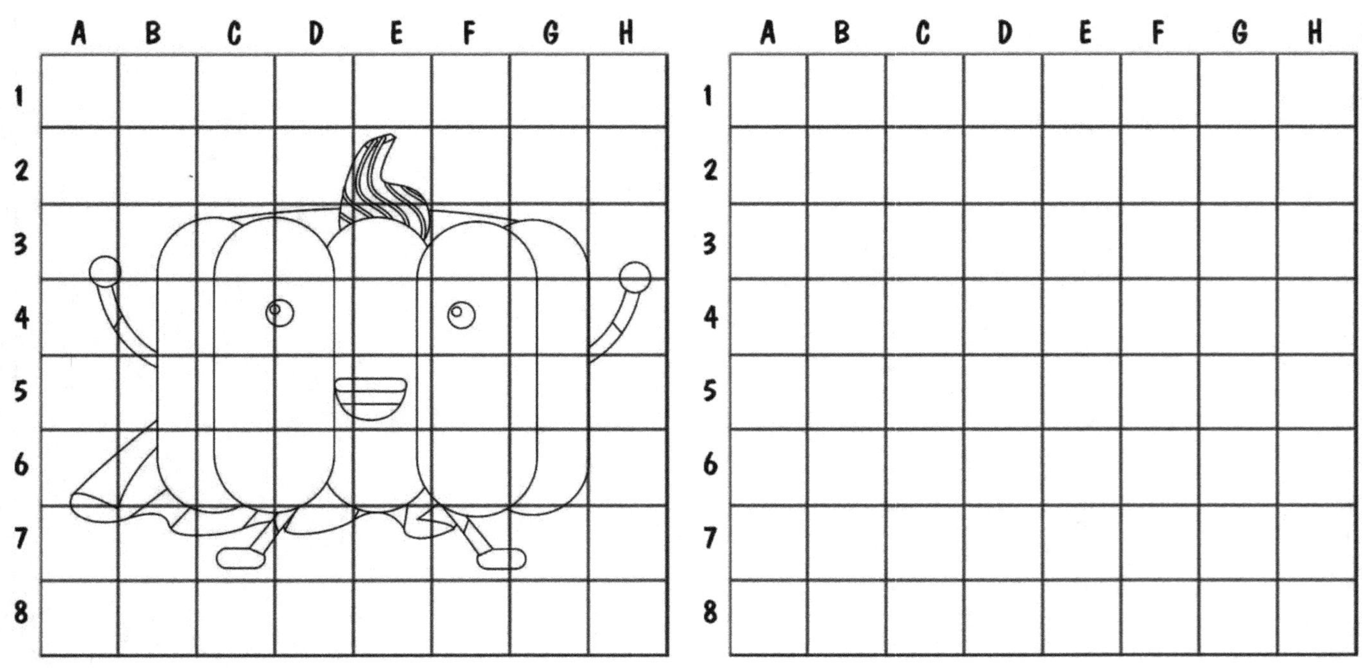

NOW COLOR IT

YOUR TURN TO DRAW

SUPER TOMATO

Step by Step Instructions

Draw inside the box with the help of art grids.

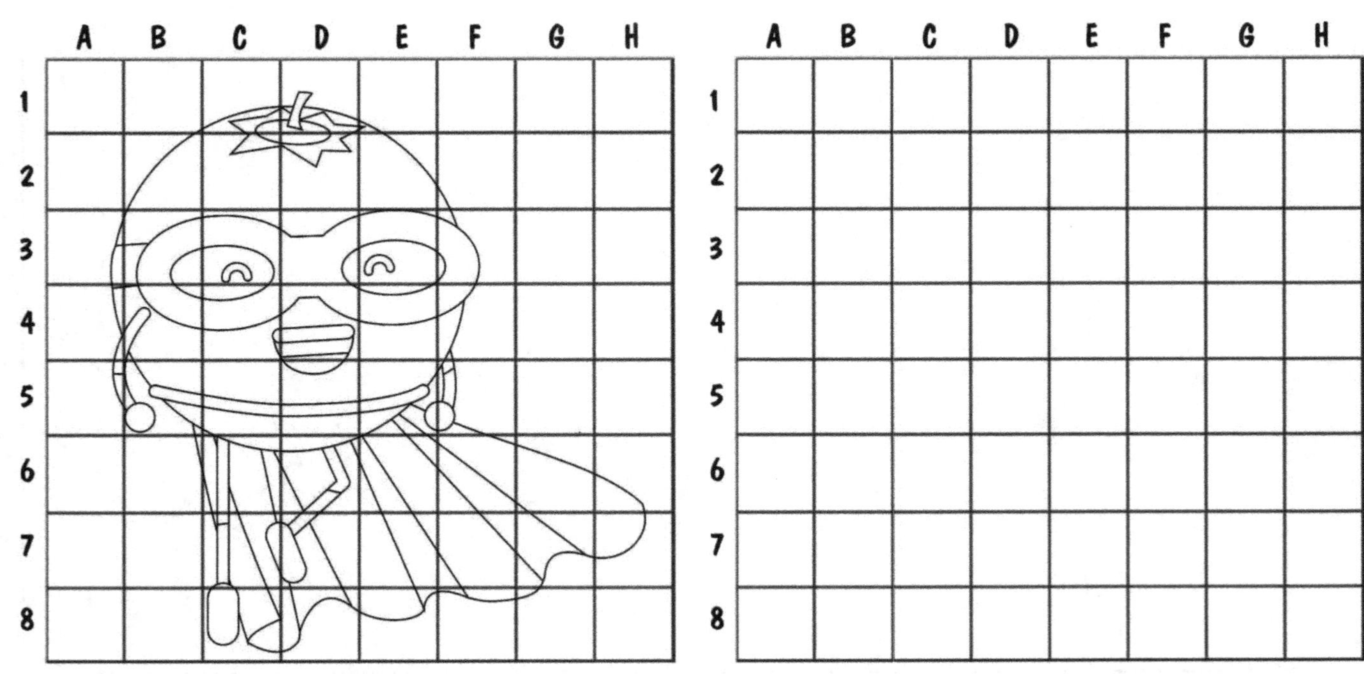

NOW COLOR IT

YOUR TURN TO DRAW

SUPER TURNIP

Step by Step Instructions

Draw inside the box with the help of art grids.

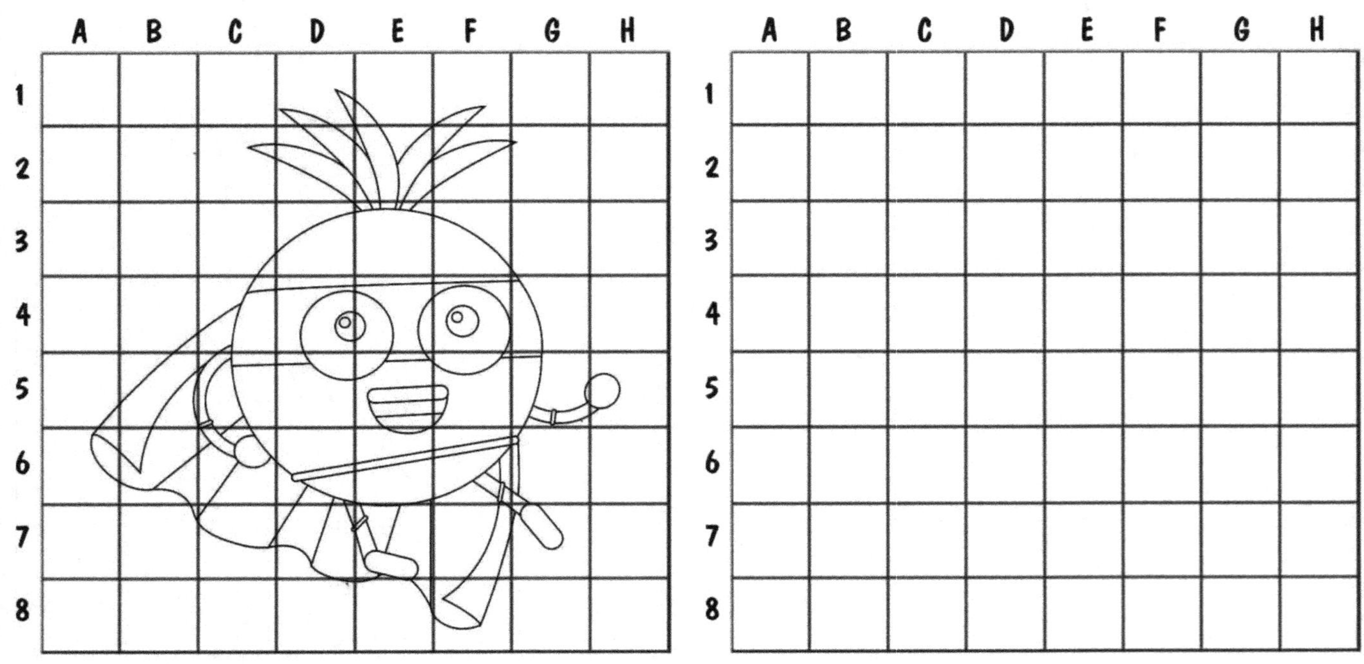

NOW COLOR IT

YOUR TURN TO DRAW

THANK YOU FOR BUYING THIS BOOK.
HOPE YOU LIKE OUR WORK.

PLEASE LEAVE A REVIEW AND LET US KNOW
WHAT YOU THINK ABOUT OUR BOOK.

FOR MORE BOOKS PLEASE CHECK
OUT OUR WEBSITE :

www.AmberForrest.com

www.ingramcontent.com/pod-product-compliance
Lightning Source LLC
LaVergne TN
LVHW060415200726

843506LV00007B/448

9788194512950